★ ★ ★

THINGS THEY DIDN'T TEACH ME IN WORSHIP LEADING SCHOOL

★ ★ ★

COMPILED BY

T●M KRAEUTER

Emerald
Books

P.O. BOX 635, LYNNWOOD, WA 98046

Emerald Books are distributed through YWAM Publishing. For a full list of titles visit our website at www.ywampublishing.com or call 1-800-922-2143.

Things They Didn't Teach Me in Worship Leading School
Copyright © 2006 by Training Resources, Inc.
8929 Old LeMay Ferry Road
Hillsboro, MO 63050
636-789-4522
www.training-resources.org

Published by Emerald Books
P.O. Box 635
Lynnwood, WA 98046

Entries in this book are taken from *Things They Didn't Teach Me in Worship Leading School* (Emerald Books, 1995) and *More Things They Didn't Teach Me in Worship Leading School* (Emerald Books, 1998).

Library of Congress Cataloging-in-Publication Data
Things they didn't teach me in worship leading school / compiled and edited by Tom Kraeuter.
     p. cm.
     "Entries in this book are taken from Things They Didn't Teach Me in Worship Leading School (Emerald Books, 1995) and More Things They Didn't Teach Me in Worship Leading School (Emerald Books, 1998)."
     ISBN 1-932096-22-1
     1. Conductors (Music) 2. Church musicians. 3. Music in churches. I. Kraeuter, Tom, 1958–
     ML3001.T44 2006
     264'.2—dc22   2006001747

Unless otherwise noted, Scripture quotations are taken from either the King James Version of the Bible or The Holy Bible, New International Version, copyright © 1973, 1978, 1984 International Bible Society. Used by permission of Zondervan Bible Publishers.

10 09 08 07 06   10 9 8 7 6 5 4 3 2 1

ISBN 1-932096-22-1

Printed in the United States of America

We, the contributors to this book, humbly dedicate these stories of our experiences to the thousands of men and women around the world who regularly lead worship in a local church. Thank you for your dedicated "front-line" ministry. We pray that you will glean both comfort and wisdom from our experiences.

CONTENTS

INTRODUCTION

~~ **A**lthough this book is entitled *Things They Didn't Teach Me in Worship Leading School*, the fact is, most people who are worship leaders (a trendy title for ministers of music) do not go to school to learn the ropes. Often these people are gifted musicians who are thrust into music ministry because of their musical abilities. If this describes you, the prayer of all of us involved in this book is that through this publication you will pick up at least a few tidbits of worthwhile ideas from experienced folks.

Some of the stories will make you laugh; others might make you cry. Some offer specific, practical help for music ministers, while others address life issues. All of the stories will encourage you to continue on wholeheartedly in what God has called you to do.

Keep pressing on and drawing near to God in worship, for "He who began a good work in you will carry it on to completion until the day of Christ Jesus" (Philippians 1:6).

Leann Albrecht

Although the name might not be readily familiar, the voice most certainly is. Leann has sung on hundreds of albums in the past twenty years. She has performed on over seventy-five Integrity worship albums  *alone, making her the voice of favorites like "I Worship You," "But for Your Grace," and "In the Arms of His Love."*

The daughter of a preacher, Leann has been touring and singing since she was fourteen. At the age of twenty she embarked on her first world tour and then shortly thereafter began recording sessions for albums and commercials. She has recorded on projects such as Women of Faith, John Tesh, Amy Grant, CeCe Winans, Steven Curtis Chapman, and Avalon, to name just a few. She has also performed with such artists as Michael W. Smith, Darlene Zschech, Don Moen, Matthew Ward, Kim Hill, Ron Kenoly, and Twila Paris.

Leann has led worship for over twelve years and has been involved with Worship International, Women of Faith, Maranatha! Praise Band, Renewing the Heart, and, most recently, Integrity's iWorship concerts. Leann was a worship leader at Belmont Church in Nashville for nine years. For the past four years she has taken a team to Italy, where they have led worship in Italian, singing songs from the Italian worship project "Lode 2002."

Leann's extensive experience, coupled with her warm personality, makes her a priceless addition to Christian music.

Right Where You Are

by Leann Albrecht

⁓ Quite some time ago I was asked to be a part of a worship team for a special service at our church. I knew that the guest speaker would probably want more singing and more personal ministry and prayer time than we normally had.

When the actual night of the service arrived, I felt very empty and needy. Honestly, church was the last place on earth I wanted to be. I was certain that I had nothing to give, nothing to offer that would benefit anyone. What was I doing up front "ministering"? The "sacrifice of praise" was far from reality to me. I was there purely out of commitment, certainly not desire.

The service began, and we led the congregation in praise and worship. Then as the guest speaker began to minister and pray for people, God moved powerfully. People were healed and set free in obviously miraculous ways. It was awesome to see!

However, as these things began to happen I became increasingly frustrated because I was bound to the microphone. All I wanted to do was get off the platform and into the nearest prayer line, but I was obligated to continue singing as part of the worship team. As the service continued on at length, it seemed as though there would never be an opportunity for the personal ministry I felt I needed.

I began to complain to the Lord about my dilemma. He quickly responded with a rebuke. In essence He said, "I am not a respecter of persons. I am everywhere at all times. Do you not believe that I can minister to you right here where you are without the laying on of anyone's hands?"

Immediately I was convicted of my shortsightedness. I had been guilty of not fully recognizing the bigness of God. Lynn DeShazo expresses it well in her song "Be Magnified," when she says, "I have made You too small in my eyes, O Lord, forgive me."

I asked God to forgive me and released my neediness to Him. I then redirected my focus to Him. As I did so, I was suddenly overwhelmed with the weightiness of His presence. The next thing I knew, I was trying to pick myself up off the floor. I had collapsed under the power of the Lord. No one had touched me or laid hands on me in prayer; it was the invisible presence of the Holy Spirit. I had never experienced anything like that before.

I began to weep as I thought of His unwavering faithfulness to meet me wherever I was, in whatever state, whatever the need! His love for me covered all of that.

Since then I have become a worship leader. This experience always reminds me that no matter how inadequate or unprepared I feel, the grace and faithfulness of the Lord will meet me wherever I am. I know that He will make up for all that I am lacking. The key responsibility I have is to keep my eyes fixed on His greatness instead of my weakness. I cling to 2 Corinthians 12:9: "For my power is made perfect in weakness."

Mark Altrogge

Mark Altrogge is a songwriter with a different flair. His particular interest and burden is to write songs of worship with doctrinal content in a style that is relevant and exciting to this generation. Around 200 of

 Mark's worship songs have been published, including "I Stand in Awe," "Forever Grateful," and "One Pure and Holy Passion." Mark has produced a series of six Scripture memory CDs called "Hide the Word," which feature over 120 Scripture memory songs written by Mark and his oldest son, Stephen.

Mark currently serves as senior pastor of Lord of Life Church, a part of Sovereign Grace Ministries. He and his wife, Kristi, have five children from ages 15 to 23 and live in Indiana, Pennsylvania. A former rock musician, he loves electric guitar in worship and anywhere else. He likes to read Puritan devotional books and mystery novels. He is a seriously frustrated fisherman, though he doesn't know enough to quit. In addition, Mark is constantly amazed by the mercy and grace of God.

THE MAN WHO WOULD NOT DANCE
by Mark Altrogge

One of the most liberating experiences for me was learning through the ministries of C.J. Mahaney and Terry Virgo about the concept of motivation by grace. But first let me give you an experience of motivation by pressure. This occurred years ago, when I was young, zealous, legalistic, and fairly stupid at times. (I'm no longer young, hopefully not legalistic, hopefully still zealous, and working on the last one.)

A friend of mine, whom I shall call Bradley, was pastoring our church. One Sunday as I was leading worship, I called upon (maybe it was more like a command than a call) the church to dance. Bradley, who shared my aforementioned qualities, looked around the church to make sure everyone was dancing. But in the back, like a lone tree in a field, stood Rick (name changed). Rick was the kind of guy you couldn't tell to do anything, especially dance. He stood there, arms crossed, staring straight ahead. Bradley could not believe his eyes. So there in the midst of a rousing celebration before the Lord, the showdown occurred. Bradley pointed to Rick and mouthed, "You— dance!" Rick just stared back like Clint Eastwood as if to say, "Make me." Needless to say, Bradley lost that battle. Rick, the lone tree, stood there for the rest of the song, arms crossed, staring straight ahead, not so much as tapping his toe.

In those days, worship leading to me was a "me-against-them" affair. I assumed that these people didn't want to worship, that they were all apathetic and complacent, and that it was my job to somehow whip them into praising God. And so, week after week, I'd exhort with phrases like, "Let's worship like we really mean it," knowing that, of course, these lazy slugs didn't mean it. I was the only one left who really loved God and really loved to worship—except for Bradley, that is. We were the remnant of true worshipers in the earth.

But later on I learned a wonderful lesson: When someone receives Jesus Christ, he or she receives a new heart; then the Holy Spirit moves and motivates that person to love Jesus. I learned that believers really do want to worship; they really do love God. God is changing them and transforming them and conforming them to His Son. Sometimes, after a week in the world, they may need a little help to get rolling, but it's not because they don't love God or want to praise Him. I found out that grace means "This I know: God is for me." God is for the people. He loves them. He can't wait to pour out His Spirit on them. Can't wait to help them.

Now, if God is so much for these people, shouldn't the worship leader be also? Looking at the people in this new way transformed my worship-leading style. Now when I encourage or exhort, I attempt to remind them of who God is and all He's done for them. God is for them, and He's a great and wonderful God. I found that when I quit pressuring people, I was somehow released from pressure myself. Worship leading became fun and the joy that God intends it to be.

By the way, Bradley's been set free too.

Paul Baloche

A *Dove Award-winning songwriter, Paul has written hundreds of songs featured on a variety of albums, including the platinum-selling WOW Worship CDs and the Time-Life Songs 4 Worship series. His many popular songs include "Open the Eyes of My Heart," "Above All," "Praise Adonai," "Offering," and "My Reward."*

Paul is an accomplished songwriter, worship leader, and producer for Integrity Music. His unpretentious and approachable worship-leading style has encouraged many to draw near to God in worship. A longtime member and producer of the Maranatha! Praise Band, Paul has traveled the world teaching and leading others in worship. He has performed in South Africa, Europe, Singapore, Australia, and New Zealand, where many of his songs have become favorite choruses sung by people of all denominations.

In addition to his songwriting success, Paul has been playing and teaching guitar professionally for over 20 years. He recently developed the Modern Worship Series DVDs, which are designed to help worship leaders and musicians expand their guitar-playing skills, equipping them to play some of the more challenging praise and worship styles of today.

Since 1989 Paul has served as the worship pastor at Community Christian Fellowship in Lindale, Texas, where he lives with his wife, Rita, and their three children.

I Want to Be a Ten-Talent Worship Leader
by Paul Baloche

In my early twenties I attended Grove's School of Music in Los Angeles, California. Grove was a one-year trade school with a contemporary approach to harmony and theory, designed to teach the skills necessary to become a "working musician." While I was there, I needed to do a lot of studying and practicing, often working for four or five hours a day at home on various things like improvising, technique, and arranging. After a while I began to be concerned that I was being self-centered and was too focused on myself and my music. I struggled with condemnation and guilt over the amount of time I was putting into "myself." I thought that I should be praying more, be involved in some kind of ministry, and be more outwardly focused. I also experienced these feelings after the praise and worship team had spent many hours rehearsing at our church.

This inner struggle went on for quite some time until, one day, a heartfelt, honest prayer of mine to the Lord became a revelation to me. I prayed, "Lord, I really want to play well enough so that I don't have to be preoccupied with what I'm doing musically. I want to be free musically to the point where I can focus on You and on the leading of Your Spirit and learn to go with the flow without being distracted by my lack of musicianship." It was one of those "aha!" moments when nothing changes yet everything changes! Although nothing had changed outwardly, I felt okay about my motives from that time on, because I knew that my heart was in the right place.

Little by little I began to realize that the investment of time I was putting into my musical education was an investment into the callings and gifts that God had given to me. The parable of the talents (Matthew 25:14–30) gives us a clear picture of God's attitude about how we invest our talents and gifts.

In this parable Jesus talks about a man who, prior to going on a journey, entrusted his property to his servants: "To one he gave five talents of money, to another two talents, and to another one talent, each according to his ability." The story tells us that the servants receiving the five talents and the two talents each doubled the money for their master. The one-talent guy, however, "dug a hole in the ground and hid his master's money." When the master came back he was very pleased with the first two. They had been faithful, and he told them, "Well done, good and faithful servant! You have been faithful with a few things; I will put you in charge of many things." But to the man who had buried his money, the master said, "You wicked, lazy servant! So you knew that I harvest where I have not sown and gather where I have not scattered seed? Well then, you should have put my money on deposit with the bankers, so that when I returned I would have received it back with interest." Then he said, "Take the talent from him and give it to the one who has ten talents. For everyone who has will be given more, and he will have an abundance. Whoever does not have, even what he has will be taken from him. And throw that worthless servant outside, into the darkness, where there will be weeping and gnashing of teeth." Yikes! That's pretty heavy! (Selah!)

I began to realize that a strategy of the enemy could be to keep God's people from pursuing excellence and keep them at a level of mediocrity. I believe Jesus is trying to tell us through the parable of the talents that God cares what we do with the gifts that He has put in us. There are many places in Scripture where God challenges and encourages us to passionately pursue our callings with an eye toward excellence.

I believe that we need to maintain our personal relationship with the Lord through quality time with Him, developing a lifestyle of worship and prayer. As the Bible tells us to pray without ceasing, our times of practicing and rehearsing and playing can be continual offerings unto God. When we spend our time and energy perfecting our skills, we can work "as unto the Lord" so that He is able to use us in strategic places to influence others toward Christ and that we might one day hear those words—"Well done, good and faithful servant."

LaMar Boschman

Creating pathways into the presence of God is the burning passion of LaMar Boschman's heart. This passion has made LaMar widely recognized as one of the trailblazers of the word of true worship throughout the earth. LaMar is profoundly grateful to have witnessed the monumental change brought by this word throughout the church world.

Founder and president of WorshipInstitute.com, LaMar has written eight books and composed numerous praise and worship songs. He has led worship on several CDs for Integrity Music and Cherub Records.

In 1986 he founded the International Worship Institute (IWI), where he now serves as dean. The IWI convenes every July in the Dallas/Fort Worth area in Texas and is the premiere institute of worship training in the world. Recent faculty members have included Jack Hayford, Darlene Zschech, Myles Munroe, Matt Redman, Paul Baloche, and other key leaders.

LaMar also serves as a personal mentor to young worship ministers and helps to promote and facilitate the worship ministry of others.

Though both Canadians, LaMar and his wife, Teresa, have lived in Grapevine, Texas, for twenty years. They have two sons, Jonathan and Jordan.

GOD WAS THERE

by LaMar Boschman

Have you ever been leading worship and were so overwhelmed with the awareness of God's presence that you lost control of your emotions? It happened to me, and I will never forget it. It was a very awkward moment—losing my composure in His presence—yet isn't that our goal?

I was leading worship at the International Worship Leaders' Institute in Dallas, Texas. We had gotten quite a ways into the song list, and everything was going great. We began to sing the passionate song "Take Me In." We had sung it a few times, and then I signaled to Tyrone Williams to begin to play extemporaneously on the soprano sax while I sang softly into the microphone and worshiped the Lord spontaneously.

As I began to hear the sax express with feeling and emotion what was in my heart, I broke and began to sob. I was overwhelmed with love for the Lord and burst into appreciation and thankfulness to Him. It so impacted me that I fell to my knees and bowed my head to the ground and cried. It was then that I sensed the presence of the Lord around me and on me. At that moment I was no longer a worship leader but a worshiper abandoned to God. There was no worship leader now; we were all in the presence of God—face to face. The service was out of the control of man. No human leadership was necessary or appropriate. Had anyone prophesied or pulled that meeting in another direction, it would have been tasteless and grossly out of order.

I remember some of the thoughts that I had as a worship leader bent over on the platform, my face wet with tears and my nose dripping on the carpet. *What is everyone else doing? . . . Should I look? . . . No, I don't want to. God, You are so awesome. I want to stay here forever. . . . Should I stand up and continue singing and leading the people? . . . Should I wait a little longer?* I finally decided to wait awhile and let the Lord finish what He had come to do. I have learned that it ruins the encounter and cuts it too short when the worship leader or pastor begins to speak direction to the meeting. Even an altar call at such a moment becomes inappropriate. The Lord is already speaking profoundly to every heart. We pray for these kinds of super-natural-power encounters, and then when they come, we often kill the moment by touching it with our great, so-called inspired, ideas. It is always my focus as a worship leader to lead the people to that kind of divine meeting with the Lord.

What does it profit anyone simply to sing songs for forty-five minutes? Worship leaders are to lead people not in songs but to Jesus. The purpose of worship is to invoke the presence of our exalted Lord.

Finally, after about fifteen minutes (which seemed like a long time as a worship leader but not long enough as a wor-shiper) I stood up and wiped my face. (Always have facial tis-sue close to the team and the congregation.) I led the people in the song again. "Take me in to the holy of holies. Take me in by the blood of the Lamb. . . ."

I noticed that the people in the congregation were on their faces too, without any direction from the platform. Slowly people began to stand up and sing with me. I didn't want to rush them. We just sang softly until they wanted to rise and sing as well.

As worship leaders, we should never force such moments into another direction or hurry the people. Transitions should always be slow in worship. When we talk after a moment like this, our voices should be soft and the spirit of our words should be that of our hearts, broken and contrite.

What does a worship leader do after this kind of encounter? Where do you go after this? What transition would be in order? My only option was to sing another soft, worshipful song or respond in prayer. I began to pray and tried to sensitively verbalize what we were experiencing and communicate to the Lord our response.

Worship's fruit is the presence of the Almighty in our lives. As worship leaders, we must be sensitive to allow God to enter our services and do what He came to do. He can even lead His people without our telling them what to do. The key is to take the time to listen to Him and follow His direction.

Steve Bowersox

Steve Bowersox is the founder and president of the Bowersox Institute of Music, a nonprofit organization dedicated to the development of the musician in worship. He is the founding executive director of Integrity  *Music's Worship International and currently serves as music director.*

Steve holds several degrees in music and business and has authored The Worship Musician's Theory Course, Vocal Aerobics: A Fitness Program for Your Voice, MIDIanites Redeemed, *and* The Worship Leaders Survival Kit. *He has toured with several prominent musicians and is proficient in wind instruments, guitar, bass, electronic keyboard, and MIDI (Musical Instrument Digital Interface).*

Steve is recognized as one of the pioneers and leaders for technology in the Church. His humor, mixed with excellent inspirational teaching, ministers to the spirit, refreshes the mind, and motivates believers to stir up their gifts. Steve travels around the world, teaching on worship as a lifestyle, leadership, and musical excellence.

Steve, his wife, Rebecca, and their daughter, Rachel, live in Jacksonville, Florida.

THE PIANO LESSON

by Steve Bowersox

The pastor asked me if I was available after the morning service for lunch. Being a bachelor at the time and considering my options, I was more than happy to accommodate. As I began to inquire, I found out we were going to a member's home to look at and listen to a grand piano we might acquire for our sanctuary. Now I was really excited. A home-cooked meal and a new grand piano! I liked the upright we had from our old building, but it just didn't fit the decor or style of our new sanctuary.

As we walked into the living room, I saw a gorgeous piano shining in the front sitting area. The room looked as if it had been built for the piano. As we exchanged greetings, the piano almost sparkled in the sunlight. The dark lines in the grain of the brown mahogany were a perfect accent to the room. The finish was so shiny and smooth it could have been used to do a commercial for furniture polish! Our hostess was in a difficult place financially, and this beautiful piano, which had been financed, was creating a real problem for her. Our church was considering the purchase of this piano to help her out and to obtain a much-needed grand piano for ourselves.

Everyone was excited and asked me to play. The truth is, I don't think I'd ever seen a piano that was as nice a piece of furniture. As I lifted the lid covering the keys, I saw a name I didn't recognize, but even the lettering was quality. I guess I didn't know as much about pianos as I thought. After all, the conservatory had only two types of pianos: Steinways and Yamahas. I knew a few other brands, but not many.

The moment of truth arrived. I was already dreaming of the melodies and harmonic lines I would play. *I'll start with something everyone knows and let this baby really sing,* I thought. I ran off an arpeggio to introduce a beautiful song. Ugh! I could hardly push the keys down. It was like moving wet cement! The sound was okay—a little mushy, I thought—but what was wrong with the action? Everyone else smiled and oohed and aahed over it. I was ready to soak my hands, and I hadn't even played one refrain! I kindly asked our hostess if she played very often. She replied that she really couldn't play but that she had always wanted a grand piano. It was actually more for show than sound. Hmm, I guess so. Well, maybe it just needed to be broken in, or maybe I had gotten soft on that old upright.

Lunch was being served. I played a bit longer as everyone was seated. The piano was a little out of tune—no matter, that could be fixed. I was running scales, playing songs I knew, showing off my best music-store licks! But, oh, was the action stiff. Was there something inside holding the keys down? No, just standard piano hammers. I finally joined the others at the table, and it seemed like someone dropped a cue and everyone looked at me and asked, "What do you think of the piano?" Uh-oh, I hadn't even eaten yet!

I answered as nicely and honestly as I could. "Uh, well, it is a beautiful piano, but it is very hard to play. The key action is really stiff, and it was a real workout to play." Someone said, "Yeah, well, it's a new piano. It should loosen up after you bang on it awhile!" We all kind of laughed and went on with the meal. Afterward, I went back to the piano to play it again. Maybe it had improved! The pastor walked in and looked at my forlorn scowl. "Steve, we really need to help her out here. She could lose everything because of the way this thing is financed." I said, "Oh, please don't buy this—I can't play this thing. It's a beautiful piece of furniture, but it is not a musical instrument. If we have to, let's buy it and give it to the Methodist church down the street!" I guess that sounded funnier than I had intended, because that got a real chuckle from the pastor. He then said something that pierced my heart, and I knew it was right from the heart of God. "Steve, the most important thing in ministry is people—our people, any hurting people. In the scope of God's master plan, this piano is really not that significant, but her life is!"

I let out a sigh. "Yeah, you're right," I said, "but this will be my instrument of worship. I will have to lead the people into the presence of God and battle this thing the whole way! Maybe it will get better; I'll get a technician out to work on it." The deal was done.

The next Sunday the new grand piano was in the sanctuary. It did look great on stage. Everyone in the congregation was excited to hear this new piano. So we took off with a "greatest hits" list of worship songs. About halfway through the list, my hands were exhausted. My fingers felt bruised, and I had broken almost every fingernail. And to make matters worse, the woman we had bought the piano from was in the front row, just grinning from ear to ear! Everyone was in a great place of worship—except me. I was angry. I was hurting. I knew this would happen. I had told them! I began to despise this piano.

This is pretty much how it went for over two years. I had a couple of different technicians look at the piano several times, and it improved slightly. Eventually the keys began sticking after I played them. They would just stay down! I would push them down, then lift them up again to push them down again. A couple of times the sustain-pedal bar just fell off the piano. I'd do one of those a cappella worship things so I could crawl underneath the piano and hook it back up! Not only that, but the piano would go out of tune during a service. You could hear it drop in pitch! I would have brought out the old upright, but someone had given it to the Methodist Church down the road. (Where did they get that idea from, anyway!)

Despite the piano, our church continued in explosive growth. Our worship really intensified, and we had many awesome times in the presence of the Lord. The woman who had originally owned the piano joined the choir and became an outstanding alto soloist. As the pastor had foreseen, she got back on her feet and was a substantial member.

From that church, I left to start a worship training ministry with Integrity Music called Worship International. It was difficult leaving my church family and friends, but we all knew this was of the Lord. Sometime after I left, the church purchased a new piano—one of those nice electronic grands by Roland. Mmm, it was nice—and always in tune!

One day I asked the Lord why I had had to deal with that old bang-n-chang piano. He told me I could have been delivered sooner if I hadn't struck the rock that God used to help His people get free in worship. Wow! I immediately saw how I had acted like Moses and had struck the rock. In Numbers 20:8 God instructs Moses to speak to the rock before the eyes of the people, that the rock would pour out water. The entire community would live from this water. But when Moses faced the people, he was irritated by their rebellion. He said, "Listen, you rebels, must we bring you water out of this rock?" Moses struck the rock, not once but twice, with his rod. God still performed the miracle, yet Moses had sinned with his anger and his pride. I think it's interesting to note that he struck the rock with his rod, which symbolizes a work of the hand or individual strength. God had instructed Moses to speak to the rock, something of the breath, which symbolizes the Spirit. In verse 12

God says, "Because you did not trust in me enough to honor me as holy in the sight of the Israelites, you will not bring this community into the land I give them." God was still honoring His promise to the people, but Moses would not enter the promised land.

Neither Moses nor I entered our promised land! For me the promised land would have been at least a new Roland keyboard. Oftentimes we see and focus on the current, short-term affliction instead of the future blessings and growth. Or we start to depend upon our own talents and strength instead of keeping our trust in the Lord.

I like God's sense of humor in my situation. He told me I could have been delivered sooner if I hadn't struck the rock. Even He called that piano a rock! The whole experience was one of growing and learning for me. I would never trade those days of worship. It was really the place and time for me to cut my teeth as a worship leader. I know that the anointing of the Lord grew on me in those days despite my attitude toward the piano. Praise God for His mercy. And I'm grateful to see the growth of the former piano owner. She really did come a long way in the things of the Lord. She even became a special friend to me. The pastor was right—people are the most important thing in ministry. God is more interested in tuning lives than in tuning instruments.

Such a valuable lesson to learn—and besides, I have really strong hands now!

Scott Wesley Brown

Scott Wesley Brown, an artist whose career has spanned three decades, continues to prove his relevancy to the changing times. A prolific song-

writer, dynamic vocalist, challenging author, international missionary, worship leader, and Christian music pioneer, he has left an indelible mark on Christian music.

Scott has recorded twenty-three albums, with nine number-one singles in adult-contemporary and inspirational music rankings. His music has been recorded by many artists, including Sandi Patty, Amy Grant, Bruce Carroll, Pat Boone, The Imperials, Mark Lowry, Petra, and international opera star Placido Domingo. Scott has been a featured singer at Promise Keepers and has written several songs for these events.

Scott's heart is mission minded. Scott has traveled to fifty countries and has worked with Compassion International, Youth With A Mission, Open Doors, Operation Mobilization, and Campus Crusade for Christ. He helped organize the first publicly promoted Christian music festival in the former Soviet Union and has delivered hundreds of musical instruments to Christian musicians and missionaries in third world and restricted-access countries.

Scott has worked closely with the U.S. Center for World Mission and Advancing Churches in Missions Commitment (ACMC), and he teaches many worship and mission seminars in addition to maintaining an active concert schedule. Scott lives with his family in San Diego, yet he serves as a worship pastor at Scottsdale Bible Church in the Phoenix area while extending his studies at Westminster Seminary. Scott received his ordination from the Southern Baptist Convention.

SKIP CHOSE JOHN

by Scott Wesley Brown

When I was in college, I served as a volunteer leader for a high school ministry called Young Life. Once a week we would hold a "club" meeting in the home of one of the high school kids who were involved with the program. There were three people who led the club: Skip, John, and I. Skip was the area director for Young Life. He had started the ministry in this particular high school and had kept it going ever since. He was a brilliant theologian and speaker, with a seminary education. His stirring gospel messages at the end of each club meeting made me want to accept Christ all over again.

John was a local college student who was quiet yet friendly. He didn't have much talent in the speaking or singing department. He basically just hung around with the kids. On the other hand, I was given charge over the song leading and cherished every moment of it. I could razzle and dazzle the kids with my guitar riffs. I felt confident whenever I spoke in front of the club and could be really funny in the crazy skits we performed each night. John seemed to stumble through his words, and he wasn't very funny in the skits.

Young Life was the ultimate for me, and I was convinced that when our leader, Skip, left to start a new club in another high school, he would leave me in charge of the existing club.

The reasons were all apparent. I could lead singing. I added lots of life to the skits. I could give a good gospel message and invitation. I was the obvious choice. But when Skip made his final decision, he chose John. I had to gasp for air. I couldn't believe it. When I asked Skip for a reason, what he told me has echoed in my heart time and time again.

"John wants to want to love Jesus," was Skip's response. I looked stunned. He repeated it again, "John wants to want to love Jesus." Then he said, "Chew on it, Scott." I've been chewing on it ever since.

What does it mean to want to want to love Jesus? What was it in my friend John that Skip chose over my ability and talent? I think that the main issue was and still is a heart for God rather than simply talent alone. Perhaps that is why, after God called Bezalel as a craftsman for the Tent of Meeting, Bezalel's first attribute listed is that he was "filled . . . with the Spirit of God" (Exodus 31:3). I believe this is foundational to all else. It comes before talent and ability. It doesn't negate talent and ability but prioritizes the "effectual calling," where there is relationship with God, over the "vocational calling," where there is service to God. Bezalel, an artist, is the first person in the Bible described as being filled with God's Spirit. This is what distinguished him from other talented artists and craftsmen of his day.

In Exodus 33 Moses didn't want to proceed into the Promised Land unless God's presence went with Israel. "Then Moses said to God, 'If your Presence does not go with us, do not send us up from here. How will anyone know that you are pleased with me and with your people unless you go with us? What else will distinguish me and your people from all the other people on the face of the earth?'" (Exodus 33:15–16).

Being in God's presence is what distinguishes Christian musicians from all the other musicians on the face of this earth. That's what makes the difference in us. No amount of strength, talent, or human charisma can replace the impact of God's presence. If God is not at work in our lives, we will never be able to operate in the full capacity of His power.

Geoff Bullock

Geoff Bullock spent his early childhood scaring the neighbors' cats and dogs with an assortment of loud, raucous instruments (piano, drums, and guitar) before graduating to the pub scene—playing loud music to deaf drunks!

For nine years Geoff has been the full-time worship pastor at Hills Christian Life Centre in Castle Hill, New South Wales, Australia. During that time he has produced many contemporary praise and worship

 albums, including his own The Heavens Shall Declare *and* People Just Like Us. *The writer of more than sixty popular contemporary choruses, his songs have been recorded by artists around the world.*

Geoff has traveled extensively throughout Australia and New Zealand as a worship leader and seminar speaker. He was the worship leader at the Australian Christian Music Conference from 1988 to 1991 and has convened the Hillsong Conference since its inception in 1987. He is also the director for the Hillsong School, located at Hills Christian Life Centre.

Geoff and his wife, Janine, have five children, and they reside in Sydney, Australia.

A WILLING HEART

by Geoff Bullock

In May of 1988 I received a call from my pastor, Brian Houston. A renowned evangelist had canceled the second half of a crusade in the Philippines, and Brian requested that I preach in his place. "Hey," I thought, "I'm a worship leader, a piano player, a songwriter, but an international evangelist? Are you sure you've dialed the right number?"

Three weeks later I found myself in a Philippine village and a strange culture with 150 fanatical Filipino high-school students who were giving up their summer holidays to run crusades. I was hot, scared, and feeling very much like a piano player, not an evangelist. *God, help!*

Early one morning we began our devotions—I, 150 Filipino teenagers, an out-of-tune five-string guitar (with antique strings), a portable organ with a rhythm machine, and a collection of ancient choruses in various languages. The worship leader in me thought, "How can we worship God with this noise?"

Five minutes later, however, nothing mattered, as the Holy Spirit fell on us and we worshiped a God who favors a willing heart far above wonderful music.

I felt humbled. These people were wonderful musicians and singers. Their worship was pure and God-glorifying. Yes, it did sound a little strange, a little out of key, but God was listening more to their hearts than their music. All of a sudden the evangelist in me realized that God didn't want eloquence; He just wanted to use me.

That night the presence of God fell on us all as we witnessed hundreds of salvations. God desires a willing heart far more than a wonderful preacher.

WORSHIP LIVE AND UNPLUGGED
by Geoff Bullock

"Just give me a microphone that works and a piano in the foldback" (that's "monitor" for you U.S. folks). I could hear my stressed voice filling the auditorium. It was 9:50 AM on a Sunday morning. The PA wasn't working. The tech crew was running around chasing leads, microphones, fuses, musicians, singers, pastors. "Oh God, the congregation is looking at us with a look of expectancy on their faces. Just give me a microphone that works and a—" hold on a second—"good morning, church!" I yelled. No microphone. No piano. I smiled at my panic and thought, *Who's in charge here?*

"Jesus," I prayed, "You said You would build your church and the gates of hell would not prevail against it."

I realized once again I had been sidetracked from the major issue. We started to sing. No microphone and no piano, but we did have a wonderful God who was on time, loves us heaps, and wasn't deaf! After the service we all prayed that God would help us to be more prepared so that this would never happen again.

I prayed, "God, please don't ever let me lose sight of why I'm here. If all else fails, You alone remain faithful and, therefore, nothing else need matter."

The next week we had a microphone, a piano, a full PA, and a wonderful service. Above all, we had the presence of God—just like the previous week!

Terry Butler

Terry Butler is a graduate of Azusa Pacific University and has been involved in worship ministry for over twenty years. He is currently an associate pastor at the Pomona/Claremont Vineyard Christian Fellowship in Pomona, California.

 Actively involved in training, encouraging, and motivating others in worship ministry, Terry participates in many of the Vineyard worship conferences in the States and abroad. His heart and passion is to see the whole body of Christ in unity, lifting up and giving glory to the only deserving One.

Among the various worship recordings he has led are Throne of Grace, Glory and Honor, and Before You Now. He has written and cowritten numerous worship songs, including "Cry of My Heart," "At the Cross," and "The Lord Almighty Reigns."

Terry and his wife have two children and live in Southern California.

THE EVANGELISTIC POWER OF WORSHIP

by Terry Butler

It seemed like a typical Sunday morning. Prior to the service there were no powerful revelations from the Lord about what would take place. I was preparing to lead worship.

As I stepped onto the platform, I noticed that one of our regular attenders had brought her husband to church for the very first time. She had been praying for him for months. He desperately needed the Lord Jesus in his life but seemed to be a long way from admitting it. His wife had gently invited him to church from time to time, but he had resisted. Now here he was, seated in the congregation.

When the praise and worship began, I couldn't help noticing that this man—we'll call him Al—seemed to be really enjoying the music. It wasn't the usual disinterested unsaved heathen scenario. I could tell that he was really trying to follow along and participate. He seemed genuinely interested in what was happening.

As the service progressed, the Spirit of God seemed to be moving among us in a gentle way. When we got to the fourth or fifth song, I looked over toward Al and noticed that he was weeping. Then something happened I'll never forget.

As we neared the end of the song we were singing, Al stepped out from where he was standing and started down the aisle toward the front of the sanctuary. When he got to the front, he knelt down. By this time he was crying very hard, and the senior pastor (my father) noticed him and moved to the front to meet him. Meanwhile, the rest of the congregation kept on singing with even more intensity. There were many who realized that God was at work in Al at that very moment. Al's wife and others close to her were crying tears of joy. There was no doubt that we were witnessing the miracle-working power of God!

At the end of the service we found out that Al had not been in a church service since he was a child. He told us that he felt the Lord powerfully touch him when we began to worship. He said that he couldn't wait to give his heart to God. He had to go to the front to kneel, repent, and pray.

As he shared with us, Al indicated that he hoped he hadn't interrupted the service. He was apparently concerned that he might have made a scene. We told him not to worry; we like that kind of interruption!

Al began attending regularly with his wife and grew in the faith. That Sunday, worship evangelism had taken place right before our eyes, before the altar call had ever been given. As we lifted our voices and our hearts in praise and adoration to the King, He drew a wayward child to His side.

Don't ever discount what God will do in *your* services as your people turn to Him in worship. He is no respecter of persons. If the Lord did it once, He can do it again. Jesus told us that where two or three gather in His name, He will be there. Let's expect Him to move in powerful ways as we worship Him.

David Butterbaugh

David Butterbaugh began leading worship shortly after he was saved in 1969. His worship-leading experience began in "soul sessions," gatherings of young people singing Scripture choruses after evening church services. Searching for information about worship led David  *from one Christian bookstore to another, only to find a lack of teaching material on the subject. Because of this, much of David's early worship leading was done by trial and error.*

The elders at David's home church in Grand Rapids, Michigan, discerned an anointing on David's life to lead the church body in worship during regular services. David did this for three years before moving to Dallas, Texas, to attend Christ for the Nations Institute. Graduating in 1980, he became part of the faculty at CFNI. He remained there for five years, leading the student body in worship and producing the annual worship tape, a project from which the body of Christ has gleaned many popular songs, such as "Ah, Lord God," "As the Deer," "In Him We Live," "To Him Who Sits on the Throne," and many others.

In 1986 David became part of the pastoral staff of Word of Faith Family Church in Dallas, leading worship in local services, at satellite seminars, and on national television. During this time he was instrumental in helping with citywide praise gatherings and the March for Jesus in the Dallas/Fort Worth area. Since May 1994 David has been ministering with Pastor Don Clowers at Grace Fellowship Family Church, a new church in the Dallas area. David was the worship leader on Integrity's Hosanna! Music recording I Will Rejoice.

David and his wife, Beth, and their three children live in Coppell, Texas.

Manure Madness

by David Butterbaugh

～❧ **B**ut the fruit of the Spirit is love, joy, peace, patience, kindness, goodness, faithfulness, gentleness and self-control. Against such things there is no law" (Galatians 5:22–23).

I was elected as a representative to the student council at a Bible school I attended several years ago. The eight of us on that council used to meet every weekday morning to pray and discuss things that were taking place in the student life and the spiritual atmosphere of the school. Meeting on a daily basis gave us all plenty of opportunity to get to know each other and enjoy deeper relationships with each other. The frequency of our meeting also gave us the opportunity to irritate each other on occasion, as growing relationships sometimes do. It was during one of these irritating times in my own life that I sought the Lord earnestly on what to do about this, and my mind reflected on something I had not thought about in years. I saw this picture as clearly as if it had been taking place at that moment, and the Lord used it to teach me a very valuable lesson.

When I was a young boy, our family lived on a farm in Dixon, Illinois, a small farming community in the north-central part of the state. My dad would plant crops and raise livestock: pigs, cows, horses, and, on occasion, sheep. We had a wonderful barn in which cows were milked, a hayloft to climb up into, and a separate shed with a large hay-storage area and shelter for the animals.

I don't remember how frequently we had to undertake one particular chore, but it seemed all too often that Dad would get out the Ford tractor with the front-end loader on it and the old green manure spreader for the delightful job of cleaning up the barnyard. The hay and straw that got trampled underfoot mixed in well with all of the "natural" sediment that accumulated there. The job of cleaning the barnyard usually took the better part of a day and involved several trips to the field with the John Deere tractor for spreading manure on the unplanted fields.

Down the gravel road to the lane we would go, sometimes freezing cold, sometimes dripping with perspiration from the heat. I always got nervous at this point, because I knew the responsibility that lay ahead of me. Once we had traveled up the lane and arrived at the field of destination, my dad would step off the tractor and stand on the tongue (the part that hitched to the tractor) of the manure spreader. From there he would adjust the levers on the front of the machine that made the rotating barrels (located on the rear of the contraption) spin. One of the levers also controlled the speed at which the contents of the spreader were fed into these whirling barrels (which had long tines attached to them) to fling the manure high into the air and spread it out over quite an area of the field as we drove from one end of the field to the other.

My job at this point was always to sit on the seat of the tractor and steer our little train toward a fence post at the other end of the field. As we moved back and forth across the field, it seemed my dad would always wait until the last possible moment before jumping up on to the tractor to turn us around. I was always frightened that he would wait too long before helping me to turn around, and I just knew we would go crashing into fence posts and barbed wire and weeds along the fencerow. Probably nobody would even come to look for us for days, as we would be lying under our tractor/manure spreader (including its contents) wreckage! But Father's wisdom always prevailed, and we always made the turn before the oncoming disaster took place. Once the spreader was empty, off we would drive back to the barn to repeat this procedure all over again until the barnyard was entirely clean of all its contents.

But the worst thing about this particular task was not the cold or the heat. It was not the fear of the fence crashing. It was the horrible smell of the "payload" we were spreading onto the fields! You just cannot imagine what would happen to my olfactory senses as we spread this horrible-smelling stuff around the farm! As we drove across the fields, with the manure spreader doing its job marvelously well, sometimes a big glob of this stuff would come slinging through the air and land on top of the tractor hood or, heaven forbid, even on my hat or in my lap! Ugh! I despised this job!

I used to look at those fields that we spread this stuff on and think that it was impossible for anything to ever grow in that soil again. I was certain that the smell alone would surely kill anything that even remotely resembled a crop! As time passed, the fields were plowed and disked and prepared for planting crops of corn, oats, and hay. The seeds were inserted under the surface dirt, where they waited for rain and sunlight. During this time I would always wonder where the smell went, for all that I could ever detect with the spring planting season was nice, fresh, clean air and the aroma of new blossoms on the neighboring trees and apple orchards.

After planting, I would sometimes ride my bicycle up the lane and look at those fields, and I just knew that nothing would ever come up after putting that "stinking stuff" all over the field. But, lo and behold, the right conditions—a little rain, a little sun, and the right amount of time—always produced row upon row of green shoots as the oats and corn faithfully made their way up through the sod into the sun! I was always amazed that after a few months we would again travel to the fields with tractors and wagons, not to put anything into or on the field but to harvest a great crop and put it into the corn-crib or the hayloft for use during the coming winter.

At this point in my praying (keep in mind, I am in Bible school when I remember this story), the picture stopped, and I found myself back on the steps in the student center, all alone with the Lord. I remembered the Scripture in Galatians that reveals to us what the fruit, or the crop, of the Spirit is. Then I gently heard the Lord speak to me and declare that it is the manure, the fertilizer of adverse experiences in life, that will cause the fruit to blossom and grow and produce a beautiful crop in my life!

I cannot always control the situations I undergo in my life. However, I can sure allow the Holy Spirit to do His precious work, even though I sometimes think the situation "stinks," in order to allow Him to move and change my character and person to be more like Jesus.

John Chevalier

John Chevalier is the founder and president of Moriah Ministries in Santa Rosa, California. He is a pastor, a worship leader, and the National Sales and Marketing Director for Worship Interactive, a ministry that equips worship musicians through multimedia technology.

With over 20 years in local church worship and pastoral ministry, John travels nationally equipping church leaders and servants to reach the full potential of their calling for the Lord. He has developed some of the most practical lessons and resources for worship ministry and leadership development in the local church.

John's deepest desire is to know and experience the reality of God and to communicate with and encourage others to seek out that reality and to experience all that God has for them. His greatest joy in ministry is to see people truly experience God's grace and accept His unconditional forgiveness regardless of their circumstances, their surroundings, or their past.

John has been the worship leader for many multichurch events, such as citywide concerts of prayer, the National Day of Prayer celebration, Celebrate Jesus 2000, Luis Palau's Festival Prayer Events, and March for Jesus. He currently writes on leadership and worship ministry for Technologies for Worship Ministry *magazine.*

John, his wife, Becky, and their four children, Sarah, Timothy, Jonathan, and Stephanie, live in Healdsburg, California.

"I Am Your Father"

by John Chevalier

It was May of 1995. I found myself on a plane headed from my home north of San Francisco to the Northeast to visit my parents. This would be different from my other visits because this time my father lay in a hospital bed, his life slowly slipping away. I had not seen him in about five years and really didn't know what to expect when I arrived.

My older brother met me at the airport, and we immediately left for the hospital. After the initial greetings and hugs from Mom, my focus turned to Dad. Others in the family had prepared me for Dad's condition, but there's nothing quite like being there to make reality set in. I remember my dad as always being very sharp mentally and pretty strong physically, especially for being just over five feet tall. Nothing much ever riled him, but when it did, look out! The man in the hospital bed was not the man I remembered. It was so out of character for him to be totally unresponsive to my greeting.

Over the next week I spent most of my time at the hospital being with Dad and supporting Mom. We almost lost my father on two occasions that week, but when it was time for me to return to my family on the West Coast, he was still with us.

I returned home with a heavy burden. Although I hadn't seen my father for years, it was as if I was about to lose the most precious person in my life. I remembered all the little things my father did for me as I grew up. The time, during a rain delay at Shea Stadium, when he found a way to get me into the bullpen to meet my favorite ballplayer. The times that he showed up when my high-school rock band would play at area dances, knowing full well that we would not be playing his favorite Frank Sinatra numbers. Memories of all the ground balls hit to me. The fishing trips off the end of our dock. The time he patiently looked for the wrench I dropped in the lake while we were working on the boat. It all came rushing back to me as if it were yesterday.

Two months went by. I was in contact with my mother almost daily until our family vacation in July. I purposed to leave my burden at home as we traveled to visit my wife's family in Southern California. As I always seem to do while on vacation, I carved out some time to visit a fellow worship leader at his church in Los Angeles. I sat in on his worship rehearsal and enjoyed the time we had together that evening. We said our good-byes, and I left the church to return to Orange County.

On my way home, my thoughts were focused on the events of that evening and my task as a worship leader. Then, from nowhere, I heard a voice, as though the person was in the car with me. The voice simply said, "I am your Father." The presence of God filled my Dodge Caravan like I had never felt it before. I recognized the voice of my heavenly Father speaking into my spirit as it came a second time, "I am your Father."

In tears, I focused on the Lord, wanting to hear more, but I didn't. I just knew that, for whatever reason, my God wanted me to feel His love for me in a powerful way. As I drove on, I noticed that the heaviness that I had lived with for months was gone. I had a Father. No matter how much I would miss my earthly father when he left us behind on earth, I had a heavenly Father who loved me with more love than I could ever have experienced in my life. Although I had been in pastoral ministry for years, I had no idea of the depth of my heavenly Father's love for me—at least not until the following day.

At about 2:30 in the afternoon I was alone at my sister-in-law's house when the phone rang. It was my mother. She said the words I had feared would come for the past three months. "John, your father just passed away." I cannot tell you what we discussed after that or how long I was on the phone. What I can tell you is that I was once again consumed with the love of my heavenly Father who cared enough for me, His earthly son, that He prepared me in advance for my father's passing. The only thought that was running through my mind while my mother spoke was the fact of how great a God we serve and how much He desires to be our Father. A real Father.

On that day my relationship with Him drastically changed. I have a God who is truly a Father to me. A Man I can look up to and admire. A Father whom, although I still blow it at times, I can obey with 100 percent confidence that He has my best interest in mind. I never really doubted the love of that Father. I knew the scriptures and the reassurance of His love through His Word. But until that day, I had never experienced the genuine love that He has for me. That same love can be experienced by all of His children. The next time you read the Bible, picture yourself as a child sitting on your Father's lap as He reads you a bedtime story. A story from His heart. A story that cost Him His own Son. A price that He paid so that He could be a Parent to us. Listen to His heart, hear His words, and be confident that the love of your Father will never cease, regardless of the circumstances of your life.

Did that affect the way I worship? What do you think?

READY FOR ANYTHING
by John Chevalier

Those of us who lead worship know the feeling we get as we leave the platform on any given Sunday morning. We

46

pray that the people have connected with God. We also know that besides the closing song, the worship team is pretty much done for the day. Well, on most days, that is.

I remember at the beginning of my ministry there was one Sunday when, except for me, our total pastoral staff was out of town. Our guest speaker that morning was our mission's intern, a young man who was preparing to enter the mission field. We had spoken during the week and discussed the details of the service. Since our senior pastor normally teaches for about fifty-five minutes, I needed to firm up an approximate time for our guest speaker's sermon. He told me that he normally spoke for about thirty to forty-five minutes and that this Sunday would be about the same.

Now, on this particular Sunday I chose to lead without my guitar and with only one keyboard player and a couple of vocalists. In addition, the keyboard player had asked to leave during the sermon to help in her child's Sunday school class. This was acceptable, since we had two services each week.

Following our worship I greeted several people while the announcements were being made and finally took my seat in the rear of the worship center for the message. About fifteen minutes into what I thought was the introduction, I heard the speaker say, "And as I close, I urge you to pray for us as we begin our mission to . . . ."

I couldn't believe it. The man walked off the platform. No prayer, no warning. I could have used a prayer, or at least some time to think about what I would do. I confidently walked up to the platform and met a congregation who was looking at me with anticipation as to what would come next. I don't think I have ever felt so alone in my life. Any musical support that I had wasn't due back for at least another fifteen minutes. I looked out at the people and grasped onto the only point I could recall my brother sharing. "I want you to consider one thing this morning," I said, sweating just a bit as I recited what had been shared. "I believe that God would have us do something a little different this morning." (I believed this like I had never believed anything before in my life. I just didn't know what that would be.) "I want you to take a moment and bow your head. This is something I'd like you *all* to do today. Please take a few extra moments and ask your heavenly Father to speak to you as you respond to the challenge laid before us. Today I feel the Lord prompting us to just sit and reflect in total silence."

I watched as the people responded, and as soon as I was confident that every eye was closed, I slowly walked down the center aisle to the back door of the worship center. Upon hitting daylight on the other side of the door, I broke into a sprint in the direction of the Sunday school department. I located my keyboard player, grabbed some extra music, and headed back into the worship center. We then, together, slowly walked up to the platform and entered into an extended worship set to close out the service. God met us there and ministered to us as we (or at least some of us) considered our part in winning the world for our Lord.

The moral of the story is simply this. Be ready for anything. When it comes to God's work, there is no way to predict how any service or event will come off. Be flexible. Be teachable. Listen to that still small voice, no matter how small that voice might seem at the time.

John Chisum

An ordained minister, Integrity Music worship artist, music publisher, producer, and seasoned songwriter, John has used his broad musical talents with great diversity for over 20 years to develop a unique catalog of work for Star Song Communications, Integrity Music, and Firm Foundation Worship Ministries. Widely known for his songs recorded

 by Christian artists Ron Kenoly, Steve Green, Larnelle Harris, The Gaither Vocal Band, Truth, First Call, The Cathedrals, and many of Integrity's Hosanna! Music recordings, John has been a long-time music industry professional in publisher, A&R, writer, and producer roles for over 200 projects.

A popular clinician in the area of worship, John has appeared in every major denominational church setting and many nondenominational venues. John is currently on tour with Integrity's Seminars4Worship and is a core instructor for Integrity's Worship Institute at the University of Mobile in Mobile, Alabama, and at Regent University in Virginia Beach, Virginia.

John has had nearly 400 songs published in his career, he has cowritten and produced eight children's and youth musicals, and he has released eight worship recordings. John continues his involvement at the local church level and seeks to fulfill his translocal call to "further wholeness and worship renewal in the Body of Christ" as president of Firm Foundation Worship Ministries.

John has been married to his wife, Donna, for 25 years, and they have a lovely daughter, Aly.

THERE REALLY IS AT LEAST ONE!

by John Chisum

   Having led worship over the years in many churches and with Hagin Ministries of Tulsa, I would never have thought that the Lord would thrust me permanently and full-time into a decidedly worship-oriented career and ministry.

Donna and I had been married for just a little over three years and had endured just about as much local-church music ministry as we could stand at the time. The first pastor I worked with as an associate pastor and music minister told me one day that he had been praying and the Lord told him it was time I left. "Gee," I thought, "why didn't He tell me first?" The second pastor allowed the youth of the church to run all over everyone. The third wasn't, by his own admission, even called to pastor. And the fourth, well, we never really got to the fourth. The pastor offered us a job in Nashville and then withdrew the offer after we'd made all the arrangements to join him there.

After these first three years of marriage and extremely difficult circumstances, Donna said to me one night, "Honey, why don't we just go to Nashville and get *normal* jobs and be *normal* people?" By that time I wasn't really sure what normal people were, but I was willing to try to learn! I often tell people that my favorite verse of Scripture during those years regarding pastors was, "There is none good, no, not one" (Romans 3:10, paraphrased).

We moved to Nashville in late autumn 1983 and hit the streets looking for normal jobs. Donna found a graphics position, and I found a paper route at 3:00 AM—no one wanted a burned-out music minister. It was less than three months later that I had my first song recorded and had signed an exclusive publishing agreement with Gary McSpadden and Bill Gaither, spinning my life into what is currently my tenth year in Christian music professionally.

Later in 1984 Donna and I were introduced to a young church south of Nashville called Bethel Chapel. Although skeptical of anything that resembled the type of churches we had cycled through the previous few years, we grew to love this fellowship, Pastor Ray McCollum, and the people who came to enjoy God's presence throughout each week. I would fill in as a worship leader from time to time, but I had no real desire to work even on a part-time basis with the worship ministry.

It wasn't until late 1988 that God's unique plan to restore us in ministry began to unfold. We had walked through a lot of restoration through the wonderful teaching of our pastor, and we had faithfully attended, tithed, and served in other capacities in the church. The Lord had begun to lovingly confront me on deeper issues of my heart: resentments that stemmed from childhood abuse and other things that I was blinded to for various reasons.

During this period I traveled to England on business and experienced firsthand the ministry of a true prophet of God—rare these days, unfortunately. I was introduced to this man by a mutual friend, but having never heard his name, I had no inkling that he was indeed the most prominent minister in attendance that evening at this particular event. Just after we were introduced, he told me that the Lord had been speaking to him about me, and he asked if we could have a word of prayer together. I thought, *Oh no! This guy is a real weirdo!* However, within thirty seconds of his prayer for me, I began to experience the most powerful visitation from the Lord I have ever known, and the impact of those moments works within me to this day.

The sum of what he spoke to me that night was a prophetic word of deliverance from not only the childhood issues of abuse but also the adult issues of woundedness and bitterness. From this trip I returned humbled and broken, ready to worship and serve the Lord in a new way.

Some months later in 1989, the full-time worship leader at Bethel Chapel stepped down for a ministry break of his own, and I was asked to fill in for him until they could search out a new full-time worship leader. I still had no intention of taking this position permanently, but on the first Sunday I led as interim, God blew the roof off, so to speak, as the congregation entered into worship on a level that had not been known by them at that time. I can take no credit for this! I don't recall praying very much or feeling the least bit spiritual as I went into that service. It was a sovereign act of God as far as I'm concerned, but the spark of that service grew into a flame that resulted in the writing of many worship songs over the next few years and the recording of five commercially released worship albums to date! I indeed became the full-time worship leader at Bethel Chapel from 1989 to 1992 and worked shoulder to shoulder with a brilliant worship songwriter, George Searcy (who wrote "Making War in the Heavenlies" and many others). The collaboration that we currently enjoy in songwriting grew out of our years together at Bethel Chapel, years that continue to bear good fruit as David Baroni carries the torch of local-church worship into the mid-90s.

I don't believe I would be at Integrity Music as a writer, worship leader, and manager of song development had it not been for the marvelous work of personal restoration that God brought to me and my wife through the local church and the ministry of a great pastor. So I now know, "There is one good— there is!" (Romans 3:10, reparaphrased by a restored man).

Phil Christensen

Phil Christensen is an author, humorist, and veteran worship pastor with a heart for equipping worship ministries. He has served as a worship development missionary in the Pacific Northwest but is best  *known for his songwriter interviews in* Worship Leader *magazine from 1996 to 2001. His "Story Behind the Songs" books can be found on the shelves of many worship leaders, and his articles have been published in* CCM, Promise Keepers, *at* Integritymusic.com, *and elsewhere.*

Phil is a big fan of Tom Kraeuter's ministry and has stolen so many of Tom's ideas that he now actually believes they are his own. It's really kind of pitiful. Phil's blog Thronetogether.com *is an extension of his ministry at Cedar Hills Evangelical Free Church in Cedar Rapids, Iowa, and a source of insight geared to praise teams.*

Phil is married to Mitzi, the Beauty Queen, and is father of three terrific kids. Okay, four. He says Dylan is doing better.

ANDY WALKS WITH ME
by Phil Christensen

"Seriously bad worship" would have been an understatement.

First, I was leading a song I loathed. It was a silly twentieth-century gospel piece called "In the Garden," which included lines like, "and the voice I hear, falling on my ear."

The band dragged lamely through the dated little waltz and never lifted their eyes from the chord charts. The vocal team hovered on the brink of giggles as they choked out, "and He walks with me, and He talks with me." The congregation, looking like bored junior high students, stared blankly at their tattered red hymnals. At least Pastor Mike managed to salvage the wasted time by reviewing his sermon notes.

And as if our journey to the throne wasn't *already* a train wreck, the worship service was about to get much worse.

In the fourth row an apparently drunk visitor began to bellow out "In the Garden" as if it were a German drinking song. His thundering voice was a cross between Gilbert Gottfried and Jerry Lewis.

He repeatedly shouted, "You guys are great! I love this!" and "This is for me!" He danced and jumped from the floor to the pew.

Yes, this was seriously bad worship, and I was eager to end it. We closed the set with a simple version of "Jesus Loves Me," but that seemed to *really* set off our visitor.

He flailed about wildly, bawling out the lyrics as if he were the only person in the world. In a way, he was; everyone else in the auditorium had stopped singing and now watched me in amusement to see what I would do.

I've had root canals that were more fun.

This little nightmare had actually started about three weeks before, when the Lord made it clear that I should lead "In the Garden." While He didn't send me an e-mail or a candygram, it was obvious enough—even a dense worship leader like me couldn't miss *that* voice.

Had He assigned me a new Maranatha or Hosanna piece, I would have obeyed Him in a heartbeat, but "In the Garden"? I'd been reading the right books and learning the right songs, and "In the Garden" didn't fit anywhere. It was neither contemporary nor classic. It was simply bad poetry set to an even worse waltz. Lyrics like "and He bids me go, through the voice of woe" were unfathomably awful, but no worse than the melody and chord structure.

I dismissed the prompting of the Holy Spirit and went about my business.

The following week, my wife, Mitzi, received a lovely centerpiece as a gift. It was a dried floral arrangement set on an opened, gilded hymnal, a book permanently opened to—you guessed it—"In the Garden." I walked past the reminder every time I entered the living room but still balked and refused to lower myself to what I considered sappy, religious fluff.

It had now been three weeks, and the Holy Spirit would not let me alone. Strangers at the grocery store were whistling "In the Garden." Randomly, several people volunteered to me that it was their favorite song. Every scripture I read seemed to mention gardens. Mitzi told me she wanted to start a garden.

Halfheartedly, I obeyed God. I condescendingly brought "In the Garden" to rehearsal, and we gave a valiant effort to spark up the little song. While we had developed a few skills at giving hymns loving facelifts, "In the Garden" was hopeless. The song was pure corn, but God had pulled rank on me.

Also in our song lineup that week was a simple version of "Jesus Loves Me," with a story to introduce it.

Now, though, the worship set was over, and our wild man was still clapping and whistling for more. It would have been no surprise if he had held up a lighter and thrown Frisbees. I put my guitar on its stand, slipped off my headset microphone, and slunk from the platform into the fellowship hall.

Glenda, a terrific woman, was waiting for me there. "I am so sorry, Phil," she was saying. "That noisy man came with my son Brady."

"It's no big deal," I mumbled politely, but I really wanted to massage my mangled ego and cradle a hot cup of coffee.

"I need to tell you something," she insisted, and her words began to jolt me quicker than any caffeine could.

Glenda explained that the young man's name was Andy. He had been in a mental institution his *entire life*. Brady rehabilitates men like Andy and had spent the past two years trying to get him ready to face the outside world. This trek to our church had represented the first big excursion into life for Andy.

My heart softened a bit as I heard this, but I was about to be changed forever by the next revelation.

Andy's therapy had included singing, and Brady had taken two years patiently teaching Andy two songs.

I heard it coming even before Glenda said it.

Andy's two songs were "In the Garden" and "Jesus Loves Me."

Glenda thanked me for being sensitive to the Holy Spirit, apologized again for Andy's interruptions, and returned to her seat. She was tearful and clearly moved by what God had done.

I began to weep too, but my tears were tears of shame and repentance. It was obvious that God had arranged this event specifically for Andy. While I had asked the Lord many times to work *through* me, today He had worked *in spite of* me. The true Worship Leader had even factored my arrogance and pride into His planning.

"This is for me!" Andy had cried joyfully about that precious time of worship. And clearly, in so many beautiful ways, it was.

But God had planted a message for all of us "in the garden" that morning. A message of tenderness. A message of pursuit. A message of measureless love.

After worship was over, Andy returned to his simple dorm room. He was filled with childlike confidence and delight in the fact that God had orchestrated those songs especially for him. Glenda and Brady drove home knowing they had just witnessed a miracle. And I, a worship leader who *should* have known better, walked away with a dramatic new understanding of how intimately God cherishes His people and their praises. For a fleeting moment I grasped the truth that the King Eternal who steers the stars with flawless precision is equally determined to move heaven and earth—and even the hearts of stubborn worship pastors—as He is to meet and embrace His children.

For He truly is the God who whispers in our ears with a voice like none other—the One who walks with us, talks with us, and tells us in ways more wonderful than we ever could imagine—that we are, in fact, His very own.

Curt Coffield

Curt is committed to "helping others worship." He has been a worship leader and songwriter for over twenty years. For four years Curt has  served as the worship pastor at Shoreline Community Church in Monterey, California. Curt loves the courageous spirit of his home church and is thrilled to be a part of what is happening there.

As a member of Integrity Music's band PK7, Curt leads worship for Promise Keeper events in arenas around the country. Curt also led worship for Promise Keeper events in 2000 with Maranatha! Promise Band. Curt has led worship teams to fourteen nations on four continents, and for two years he traveled as a clinician for Maranatha's Worship Leader Workshops.

Curt's songs have been recorded by a variety of artists and groups, such as Israel and New Breed, Maranatha! Praise Band, Willow Creek Community Church, and Christ for the Nations Institute (CFNI). Some of his most noted songs include "All Around," "You've Won My Affection," "Still I Will Worship You," and "Just a Glimpse."

In years past Curt served as worship director at Willow Creek Community Church in South Barrington, Illinois, and as worship leader at Resurrection Life Church in Grandville, Michigan. While at Resurrection Life, Curt led worship on three live recordings.

Curt lives in Monterey with Jennifer, his bride of fourteen years, and their daughter, Gabbi. Jenn is a noted vocalist and worship leader who has recorded and traveled with Maranatha! Praise Band. She is now savoring every moment of being a mom and is often found singing around the house and at local parks, the beach, and the Monterey Aquarium.

The Toilet Paper Tale and Other Humble Happenings

by Curt Coffield

I'm sure you know the feeling. It comes in like a flood. The progression can go something like this:

"Oh, wow, people are laughing. Something *must* be funny. I wonder what's so funny. Are they laughing at *me*? What about *me* could be that funny?"

Then comes "the moment." It's the moment you discover what is so funny about you. I've known this feeling too many times to number.

One particular evening we were having a guest speaker. The church was packed with upwards of two thousand people, and the worship had been extra exciting. Following the worship, I left the platform, briefly visited the restroom, and then proceeded to find my seat next to my wife near the front.

It started with a snicker but quickly gained momentum. As I walked down the aisle, the laughter claimed me as its subject. It was not until I reached the front of the auditorium that I successfully completed my investigation as to the reason for the outbreak. I glanced down and discovered that a piece of toilet paper had married itself to the heel of my shoe and had followed me into the service. It had been sailing in the wind like the tail of a kite, coming in at a whopping thirty inches long! And, oh, was it comical!

It so shocked me that I instantly shook it from my shoe as one would shake off a snake going in for the kill. My wife

Jennifer's eyes reflected my horror as I sat down next to her. I rattled off what had just happened, and she, fighting off the urge to join the laughter, asked the obvious question, "Where is it now?" There it sat in the aisle, a memorial to the humility it had just so matter-of-factly handed out. I later learned that a faithful usher had humbly come to my rescue and discretely removed the troublemaker from the service.

So what's the point? The point is: *embarrassing things happen to worship leaders*. These embarrassing things have a purpose in our lives. Would you believe that eventually it's possible to become immune to embarrassment? I don't want to get into a deeply challenging theological debate over whether or not God sends embarrassment. I just know that out of these situations God can cause humility to grow in us. Humility is vital to being effective in our effort to lead others into being honest and real in their adoration of our Lord.

The truth is that as worship leaders we are continually in the place where mistakes, goofs, and mishaps occur. Accept that! Don't allow the American mentality of perfectionism to have its way. We must put aside the self-consciousness that keeps us from the ability to keep others focused on the Holy Spirit, even when we blunder. We have to come to the place were we allow others to see our weaknesses without being ashamed.

So you forget the lyrics or start the wrong song or break a string or mischord or start the song too fast or too slow. Is the focus now on you as you attempt to deal with the damage done to your ego, or do you allow God to bring you to the place where those things no longer undermine your confidence?

Please don't misunderstand the point. I'm not encouraging you to ignore these situations or to act as if they're not happening. I'm not asking you to dismiss the need for excellence. I'm not even telling you to "get through." I'm begging you to take a step back, embrace the reality of worship, and realize how unimportant our image is in this thing. People need someone real to lead them in their worship.

Don't fall into the trap of our day: an obsession with image and perfection. We frequently elect government officials on image. We buy music, often not for the artistry of the music but for the image of the artist. Allow your image to become less and less important. Our desire is to see people worship God because He is God, not because of a certain persona that we can simulate.

Resist such thoughts as "Oh no, people must think I'm a geek," and embrace the Lord. Our prayer should be, "God, I'm willing to be whoever I need to be and look however I need to look, if it makes You more real and reachable in worship."

I'd like to be able to say that I have totally mastered this discipline, but I can't. This willingness to place ourselves in vulnerable positions in serving our congregation can go beyond the borders of worship. About two years ago the director of Women's Ministry at our church asked my wife and me to sing for the "Ladies' Spring Tea." With reservations, I reluctantly agreed. As the event grew closer, the reality began to set in that I would be the only guy in this group of four hundred women.

Things got worse. We were asked to sing "Don't Sit Under the Apple Tree with Anyone Else But Me," a song from the '30s! My mind began to work: "What will people think? I'm a worship leader. I never signed up for *this*! This is *not* me." Have you ever caught yourself with such thoughts?

The evening came. I tried to disguise my negative attitude as best as possible. Jenn and I sang, and then I jetted from the building eager to reclaim my masculinity. Thank God for His grace that redeems us from such self-centeredness. The next week I was walking through the church, and Mary, a beautiful grandmother and saint of the faith, took me aside to tell me what the experience had meant to her. Mary is one of the most encouraging people in all of the church. She's always there in services with her hands raised to God, pouring her heart out to Him in worship. No matter how new and contemporary the chorus, she never misses a beat.

Here I stood following the "Tea," with Mary, teary-eyed, sharing how special the song "Don't Sit Under the Apple Tree" was to her. She explained that it was her and her husband's favorite song when they were dating, and it had been years since she had heard it. She had appreciated hearing me and Jenn sing it, as it had brought back such special memories.

There I stood—*stunned*. Do the words "subtle Holy Spirit rebuke" mean anything to you? To think that such ministry could occur in such a vulnerable, seemingly embarrassing place! God broke something in me standing right there in the hall. I literally fled to my office and cried before God, asking Him to remove the pride of my heart. I truly believe that through this incident God "grew" me in my effectiveness as a worship leader, helping me to become more immune to this sense of embarrassment.

I recall the time that Jenn and I were leading in the worship band at CFNI. We had been out of school for six years and were so honored to be asked to come and lead worship for the student body. As we were worshiping, my guitar chose to release these "yells from hell." I fought the temptation to think, *These kids must think, "What an idiot—get a real guitar."* Instead I tried, in God's grace, not to become crippled with embarrassment and thus be rendered ineffective. I simply continued to worship God. Later I realized that it was actually beneficial for those students to see that times of worship don't always go perfectly and that in those moments we can still continue to stay focused on God and our desire for more of Him.

Then there was the time we were opening a service with David Baroni's song "Ain't Gonna Let No Rock." What a great song! We had always started the song with a slow verse first. I got the bright idea to start it in the middle of the chorus, a cappella (trust me, don't try it). Walking out on the platform, Karen, our choir director asked, "Where will we get the pitch for our first note?" I confidently said, "I'll strum out the chord and we'll get it." I sang out the first note, with the choir and ensemble joining in hopeful confidence, but by the second chord it was obvious we were miles away from the real key. I pulled the whole thing to a stop and started again . . . with the same result. It was another opportunity to become crippled with embarrassment. Instead, it became a moment of being real and not overly "slick." I took a moment to allow everyone to laugh about the obvious. I shared my heart for a moment, being real and not overspiritualizing the situation. It was a true moment of bonding with our congregation. We eventually started the song, and I'll guarantee no rocks cried out for us that night. An experience that could have sent at least those on the platform home for the evening instead displayed our realness and made the platform feel less like a stage.

Be willing to laugh at yourself. Be willing to be real. Take on no sense of image or mystique. Take on Christ and His willingness to become but a servant that others may know God. By the way, on the night of the adorning toilet paper incident, I returned to the platform at the end of the night to lead into worship those who had been laughing. I can honestly say I was not hindered by the incident. Instead, I added to the numerous other stories of how God causes us to grow in our service to others in order to serve Him.

Lindell Cooley

Raised a preacher's kid, Lindell Cooley had seen all that religion had to offer... and he wasn't impressed. However, he had witnessed the reality of God, and his spirit responded to God's call at an early age.

A self-taught musician, Lindell improved and matured his talents through hard work, encouragement from friends, and on-the-job training at his dad's church.

At the age of fourteen Lindell felt the Lord tell him that he would be used to take music around the world. Despite the seeming impossibility of such a thought, the strong sense of destiny to that end never departed. Lindell became an accomplished musician with many accolades to his credit, but it was nearly twenty years before God plucked him from obscurity and placed him at Brownsville Assembly in Pensacola, Florida. He has been the music minister at Brownsville since the spring of 1995.

In 1997 Lindell founded Music Missions International, a ministry to spread the gospel of Jesus to the world through ministry, music, and missions endeavors.

Lindell, his wife, Amber, and their son, Samuel, live in Pensacola.

THE NIGHT THE ANGELS SANG
by Lindell Cooley

~*V*ery early in the revival at our church we noticed supernatural occurrences in the worship service that let us know that God was personally involved in this revival, even in areas not related to the hundreds of souls won each night. I looked in my personal journal and found an entry dated August 17, 1995 (about two months after the revival began). This is what happened:

The service that night seemed to be pretty average until the very end. As I was about to leave, I talked with Richard Crisco, the youth pastor, and he questioned me about a particular worship chorus we sang toward the end of the service. It was an ad-lib song that we had sung spontaneously. He wanted to know how I was able to cue the soundtrack tape to come in as precisely as it did. I told him there was no tape; it was just me and the keyboard—there weren't even any singers. When I explained this to him, he didn't believe me. He said that he had heard at least three voices and several instruments.

As Richard spoke, I remembered that I too had heard another voice singing a beautiful countermelody but was so caught up in worshiping the Lord that I didn't see who was singing. I knew I was singing, and I assumed it was Jeff Oettle (one of the worship singers at the time) or someone else who had grabbed the microphone to join in.

As Richard talked, I also remembered hearing a third voice come in that was singing a perfect countermelody to my song. The third voice was exceptionally clear, and the countermelody sounded rehearsed. That should have been impossible, since I was making it up as I went along. Yet this voice was singing a perfect countermelody with amazing clarity at the same time I was singing.

Later on, the sound engineer and the children's pastor told me that they had heard the third voice too. They were at the sound board and were trying to find out what channel the third voice was on. (It wasn't coming through the sound board at all!)

Later that week I asked Jeff Oettle, "Were you singing with me?"

"No, but I was standing onstage."

Then I asked him, "Did anybody else sing with me?"

I already knew the answer. "No."

My conclusion was that the voices were definitely not of this world.

Two girls from Puerto Rico who had backgrounds in witchcraft had come to the revival that night. When I started singing this song, hundreds of people were still being prayed for at the altars, at which time it is normally pretty loud. However, as this song began, accompanied only by the keyboard, everything became totally quiet. The song, with the heavenly voices, was so impressive that everyone stopped to listen. (Everybody I questioned that night heard it.) This lasted for probably two or three minutes.

When I stopped singing, one of the Puerto Rican girls sitting to my far right released a bloodcurdling scream, and I thought, *How rude of you to interrupt.* But it was as though a demon had left. The girl told one of the intercessors who was working with her that she had tried to get deliverance from the witchcraft that she had practiced for years, and she'd never been really free of it. Once the angels had started singing, that demon left her, and she was totally free.

Adapted from Lindell Cooley, A *Touch of Glory: It's Your Destiny* (Shippensburg, Pa.: Revival Press, 1997). Used by permission.

Tommy Coomes

Tommy Coomes was a pioneer of contemporary Christian music in the 1970s as a member of the band Love Song and was a record producer and the creative director at Maranatha! Music in the '70s, '80s, and '90s. He produced or executive produced several hundred recordings, including the popular Praise Series.

Tommy loves to innovate, create, and influence the church to worship and witness. He founded the Praise Band in 1989 to explore new forms of worship and evangelism and has ministered around the world with Franklin Graham, Billy Graham, and Greg Laurie's Harvest Crusades.

Tommy pioneered the Maranatha! Music Worship Leaders Workshops in 1991 to train and equip the church in contemporary forms of worship. In 1992 he formed and led the Maranatha! Promise Band to serve the growing Promise Keepers movement.

As a speaker, teacher, and consultant, Tommy draws on a depth of experience as a singer, songwriter, producer, performer, and worship leader. His greatest joy is "to know Him and make Him known." Tommy and his wife, Shelley, live in Southern California with their two sons, Tyler and Erick—both musicians.

His ministry statement is reflected in Psalm 40:3: "He put a new song in my mouth, a hymn of praise to our God. Many will see and fear and put their trust in the LORD."

Looking Past the Differences

by Tommy Coomes

~ **D**uring the early 1970s I was privileged to be a part of Love Song, one of the very first contemporary Christian music bands. The members of this group were tremendous musicians and singers. Some had previously opened for groups like Three Dog Night and Grateful Dead and had had several hit records. We were all in our early twenties, and we all had one other thing in common: very little experience with church.

We found Christ in a small, informal church called Calvary Chapel in Costa Mesa, California. Pastor Chuck Smith Sr. and his wife, Kay, had a tremendous heart for young people. Many kids in their teens and twenties were coming to the Lord and being baptized in the Pacific Ocean. The media called it "The Jesus Movement."

Love Song was a contemporary Christian group, but worship was always a big part of our ministry. I wrote the first worship song recorded by Maranatha! Music and produced the Praise Album Series. Chuck Girard, another member of Love Song, has written many great worship songs and continues to sing and teach around the world. Helping others find Christ and worship Him was what we were all about. It's still what we are about!

Psalm 40:3 declares: "He put a new song in my mouth, a hymn of praise to our God. Many will see and fear and put their trust in the LORD." That was our experience. God changed our lives. His Spirit put a new song in our hearts. But this "new song" was also in a new form that many "churched" people had to stop and think about. Was it genuine? Was it sacred? Was it secular?

We experienced a variety of responses to our "new song." Many were saved. Many wrote us off. Some would weep, while others found new joy. Some were confused and fearful. New things are often messy. We were young and naive and had some lessons to learn about God and about His people. One of the greatest lessons we learned came out of one of our greatest personal rejections.

We were only a few months old in the Lord when a Bible teacher informally invited us to sing at a Full Gospel Businessmen's Convention in Oakland, California. I'm not sure what we expected to find at the end of our four-hundred-mile drive, but we were shocked. It was suits and ties, chiffon dresses, and hair spray as far as the eye could see. (Remember, this was the early '70s!) We, on the other hand, looked more like where we had been than where we were going.

When we walked into this formal setting, it reminded me of the parting of the Red Sea. We were so out of place that everyone immediately started moving away from us as fast as they could. It was apparent that these people did not want us at their "nice" convention. They were rude to us. Unfortunately, we were quick to privately criticize their actions. We had not experienced anything like this in Southern California. The older, more conservative Christians there had welcomed us and were happy that our lives were changing.

It should be understood that every kind of radical, political, and antiestablishment faction imaginable was alive and well in this (the S.F. Bay) area during the late '60s and early '70s. What we didn't know was that one of these militant groups had disrupted this same meeting the year before.

The head of the convention—we nicknamed him "Cool Hand Luke"—was afraid that we represented a new disruption and made it very clear to us that this was *his* convention and that he had no intention of letting us sing. It didn't matter who knew us or who had invited us!

After two long days of rejection and growing disdain, we found ourselves at a Sunday-morning prayer breakfast. An impromptu meeting was being held by the leaders and speakers at their long table at the front of the ballroom.

It was funny. It looked like a football team in a huddle. Every once in a while someone would peek out and point back to the corner where we were and then go right back into the huddle. The speaker who had invited us was asking Demos Shakarian for his permission to let us sing that morning. A messenger appeared from the huddle and walked toward us. "Why don't you get your guitars and be ready to sing one song," he said.

As we approached the platform, Cool Hand Luke was there to greet us. He was not happy that someone had gone over his head. He grabbed my arm so hard that I thought he would break it. He looked me in the eye, gritted his teeth, and said, "One song and no talking." I was shaking like a leaf! I was just a few months old in the Lord and didn't understand the politics and power struggles that were going on. I just wanted to sing for Jesus.

We filed onto the stage with two acoustic guitars and a violin and formed a semicircle around the lone microphone. I'm sure the people in the audience were wondering, "Who let these guys in here? How did they get on the stage?" We sang one song—"Welcome Back."

As we began to sing, something happened that I've never seen before or since. As I looked out over the large room full of people, it appeared as though a wave was rolling from the right side of the room to the left. I live in California near the ocean, where I'm used to watching the waves roll in. This was a wave of the Holy Spirit. People began to weep as He touched them.

It was as though eyes were suddenly opened. We were all able to look past the outward appearance. The Bible says, "Man looks at the outward appearance, but the LORD looks at the heart" (1 Samuel 16:7). People saw God at work in a way that they didn't expect. Suddenly everything changed.

Cool Hand Luke quickly appeared and asked us to share our testimonies, one at a time. It took twenty minutes. Then he asked us to sing a second song.

Bob Mumford was the guest speaker that day. He gave us a great lesson on God's secret weapon: agape love. When people don't love you, just pull out your secret weapon and love them anyway.

After the service was over, I witnessed one of the most amazing demonstrations of the miracle-working power of God's love I have ever seen. A five-foot-tall white woman with silver hair approached a very tall black man with a huge Afro. As she reached up to hug this six-and-a-half-foot former Black Panther, who was now a new Christian, she looked straight into his eyes and said, "You know, before today I could never love anybody that looked like you." Tears filled their eyes and mine.

God removed the veil from all of our eyes that day. We learned that His love is able to do things that we cannot do on our own. We began to understand that His love is what binds us together. It's His love and Spirit that we must look for. Our job is to serve Him. People are afraid of change. We should expect that, but at the same time we must pray for God to build a bridge by His Spirit. We have seen Him answer that prayer over and over again.

There may be people in your church who look different or act differently than you. You might not like them. They might not like you or your music. However, God has called us to love. That love goes beyond all outward differences.

I'll never forget the lesson we learned that day in Oakland. It has guided me every day of my ministry. I still have the audio tape of that morning's service. The label says, "Testimony of Converted Hippies"! It also says, "God's Secret Weapon."

Shawn Craig

Shawn Craig has served in music ministry for over eighteen years. A prolific songwriter, he is probably best known for his song "In Christ Alone," which won the Dove Award for Song of the Year in 1993. As a member of the contemporary singing group Phillips, Craig & Dean, he has traveled extensively throughout the United States, ministering in churches of various backgrounds.

Shawn is also the author of a devotional book called Between Sundays, *published by Howard Publishing.*

Shawn currently serves as worship leader and music pastor for South County Christian Center in St. Louis, Missouri.

GOD IS NOT SURPRISED!

by Shawn Craig

When I read chapters 3 and 4 of the book of Exodus, I can't help but smile a little at Moses and his doubtfulness. God chose Moses to be the leader of a nation, yet Moses seems to be more than a little surprised at what God is calling him to do: "What if they do not believe me or listen to me?" (Exodus 4:1).

The reason I smile when I read this is that I see myself in the calling of Moses. In fact, I never cease to be surprised at the way God has continued to expand my vision along the way.

As a teen I knew that God had called me to some sort of full-time service. But the only evidence of gifting was my love for music. I would practice singing and playing for hours, with dreams of being an accomplished musician. My time with the Lord was often filled with a hunger for His presence, but I had no definite sense of how my love for music would fit into God's plans for my life.

I recall one older saint saying to me, "Keep up the consecration, son. One day you will preach the Word." I remember thinking, "What a confused lady. I know my gifts and I know my limitations. She recognizes God's calling on my life but obviously doesn't know I am called to be a musician."

As a young man in Bible school in central California, I studied music and began to realize that not only could I continue in music but also music could be a ministry. I took a part-time job in a local church and was thrilled to be involved in music every day, even though it was a struggle financially. I remember a lot of PBJ sandwiches. My greatest struggle, though, came with the leadership aspect of being a music director. Because of my own lack of self-confidence, I found it most difficult to bear the responsibility. I felt unequipped and unworthy of the call. Yet God seemed to add to instead of take away the challenges.

A couple of years after my tenure at that church, I discovered the renewal that was taking place in praise and worship. It was like a wonderful breath of fresh air. I loved the new choruses and the passion with which people sang. The songs I heard were much different from those to which I had become accustomed, but I loved the lyrics. They were so intimate toward God. They were less Body-directed and more Christ-centered. I knew there was much more for me to learn, and I sensed God calling me onward.

The journey from musician to music director to worship leader was a difficult one for me. Each time that I sensed the Spirit moving me out of my comfort zone, I would resist. Each new challenge would take me by surprise, and I would be aware of my own inadequacies. But with the help of supportive pastors and friends, I would cautiously walk through each new door. God would meet me each time, giving me the ability to take each leap of faith.

Soon I found myself entering a new reality in worship. I began to experience a wonderful flow of the Spirit in my personal devotion time as I worshiped at His feet. It wasn't long before I had an overwhelming desire to help others experience the power of true worship, pointing them to a Christ who wanted not only to save them but also to enjoy them, to love them intimately.

Now I find myself not only leading praise and worship but also teaching and preaching—something that dear older saint had told me years ago I would do, though I could not envision it at the time.

I recall a dear one who asked for prayer after one midweek Bible study. With tearful emotion the woman said, "I don't know what to do. My children are grown and have their lives. I knew my purpose when they were at home. I worked hard to raise them in the knowledge of the Lord. Now I don't know why I'm here. What is my purpose now? I can't believe I'm at this point in my life."

I remember feeling compassion for what she was going through and, in a few moments, hearing that small voice inside saying, "Tell her that I am not surprised." As I realized the depth of the meaning in those few words, I found great comfort for her and for myself. Although at times we are surprised at the circumstances of life or the call of the ministry, God is not. He is always ahead of us, preparing the way, ordering our steps, and He is never taken off guard. Never will we hear Him say, "What will I do now?" Instead, He lovingly looks at us and says, "Walk on, child. I know you're surprised, but I saw it coming, and you are going to be just fine!"

God continues to stretch me. Now I say with joy, "Stretch on, Lord." He will continue to stretch you if you allow Him to. When your ministry is in His hands, anything is possible. If you are walking in covenant with God, He will be faithful to meet you at a point just beyond your own self-imposed limits. He knows where you are. He knows the path you take. He is not anxious or weary. "The steps of a good man are ordered by the LORD" (Psalm 37:23).

O Father, Your ways are higher. It is good to know that although I may be surprised once in a while at my circumstances, You are never shocked or startled at life. You know the path I take, and I cannot escape from Your presence. I know You have good plans for me.

Danny Daniels

Danny Daniels cut his teeth in the music industry as the key song-writer for the man who put the Righteous Brothers on the map. Danny is a veteran of Christian music and ministry, starting in the Jesus  *Movement in the early '70s and continuing as a founding member of the Maranatha! Music group Bethlehem. He has served as a staff pastor and worship leader at Vineyard fellow-ships in California and Colorado and has traveled the U.S. and abroad as a worship leader and conference speaker for Vineyard Ministries International.*

In 1993, feeling the call back to his deep roots in American music—blues, jazz, folk, country, and rock & roll—Danny recorded Another Shade of Blue *and got back on the road, performing nearly 200 dates a year in roadhouses, on coffee-house stages, in churches, and in any other venue he could find. Danny's faithful following has supported him ardently into the 2000s. With his newest release,* Leavin' on the Special, *on top of his powerful live performances, Danny has steadily grown into a modern blues powerhouse.*

Danny and his wife, Cher, live in Aurora, Colorado.

WORSHIP MEASLES

by Danny Daniels

A new Bible study was going to start in the home of some of our friends. We lived just down the street, so we were looking forward to attending. After all, it would be a pleasure to be able to walk to any kind of church function, especially in Southern California, where you drive everywhere!

A week or two before the study was to begin, the teacher asked me if I would lead worship. I had been a believer for only about three years, but I had been involved in music professionally in the studio and onstage for fifteen years. I knew that the songs, mostly choruses in those days, were not really musically challenging, so I agreed to lead worship.

After picking out six or eight of the songs that I enjoyed singing at our church, I went through them to make sure I knew the chord progressions. I "rehearsed for the gig," as I had learned to do for years. Having prepared myself and the material in the best way I knew, I felt ready to lead worship. In fact, I felt very confident that I could do a good job, because at the time I had been rehearsing several hours every day with a new band.

The night arrived. The people arrived. I arrived and was introduced as the worship leader of the evening. We all seemed to anticipate a good time of singing to the Lord. I began the first song. It seemed like I was the only one singing, because everyone else was singing so softly. Some people were just looking around. Others looked at me like I was supposed to do something. What was going on?

We finally made it through the first song, and I decided I would close my eyes and get into the songs whether anyone sang or not. Then I realized that most of the people weren't keeping tempo, and their phrasing of the lyrics was terrible. Didn't anyone know how to sing with all his or her heart? Why try at all if you don't give it all you've got? What was wrong with these people? How could I work with a group like this!

About four or five songs into it, I opened my eyes. The people were singing basically the same way, but what I saw was really different than when we started. Although the singing wasn't much stronger and the phrasing was just as loose, something was going on! Many folks had their eyes closed. Some were crying. Several had lifted their hands. They actually seemed to be enjoying this! How could that be, when it was so musically not together?

After the last song, I went out into the backyard. I was exhausted, frustrated, and generally miserable. What a mess! I looked up and said, "Lord, that was one of the worst experiences I've ever had, and I never want to do it again! I'll just stick to concerts and recording and leave that to someone else. At least I know how to worship You by myself!"

I couldn't believe what God clearly said to me, "You will be doing that the rest of your life."

"Whaaaat?" I responded. "That was terrible! Those people couldn't keep time or sing together to save their souls! I don't want to do that ever again."

"The people were fine," God said. "They even worshiped Me in spite of the fact that you don't know how to lead them yet. But you'll get better."

"I'll get better?" I thought. "I did the songs right! What are You talking about! Is this really You, Lord?"

Well, it really was the Lord. And I really didn't know how to lead worship yet. Oh, I knew the songs, the chords, and the melodies. I even kept time well. But I was still to learn that leading worship isn't just about music. It's about worshiping God with all your heart, mind, and strength while drawing people into an experience in the Spirit. It's about helping people to be themselves before God so that they can discover how much He loves them.

God put me in situations over the next several months where I could see and experience the ministries of effective worship leaders. They were each a little different and uniquely themselves, but they all showed me that it isn't just music that makes a good time of worship singing. No matter how great the singing and no matter how tight the music, without surrender and passion for God, worship does not happen. It's kind of like measles. If you've got 'em, someone can catch 'em. But if you don't, no one ever will! I'm still learning twenty years later that a worship leader must be a worshiper first, and then others may be able to come into that dimension of worship that must be caught, not taught. My goal now? Give everybody worship measles.

A FIRST-CLASS, THIRD-WORLD LESSON
by Danny Daniels

While on a trip to South Africa with a team from California, we attended a Sunday-morning worship service at a Zulu church. We arrived about 9:00 AM and were met by the pastor in a side room. He told us that the service had begun at 8:00, but we were welcome to come in and join in the singing of worship songs still in progress. Most of us were used to singing worship songs for twenty to thirty minutes in Sunday-morning services, so we were interested in what it was like for a congregation to worship in song for what was to us much longer than normal.

The congregation was singing very intensely, with a lot of clapping and many raised hands. We entered through a side door, and most of us sat in the back of the room. The first thing I noticed was that every person I could see was singing with all his heart. I could see no one who was looking around, being silent, or not participating. As I looked at this group through the eyes of a worship leader, I was struck by the great level of commitment that the people had.

Most of the songs were sung in Zulu, or as I was to find out later, Zulu and Sotho, the two primary languages that represented the members of the church. Some songs were sung in English.

Even more interesting than the large percentage of participation in singing or the songs being sung in three languages was the way that the worship musicians were set up. Most of us spend a lot of time, energy, and money to develop people, equipment, and programs that will help our churches to have meaningful, consistent worship in our services.

Though I have been to several countries and have seen variations in how different churches conduct their music and worship programs, I had never seen anything like this. The only instrument on the platform was an electric piano, which was in desperate need of tuning. Although that is not as uncommon as one might think, the fact that the person who led the singing and began each song was not even on the platform was something that I had definitely never seen anywhere.

At the beginning of each song, the keyboard player would play a chord and let it ring out until the leader began to sing. Then the people would either pick up the song with the leader or answer with a countermelody or lyric. This wasn't something that was new to us, but the fact that we couldn't see the leader on stage was.

I tried to find the source of the voice through several songs. It was a female voice, full of emotion and passion. In fact, this woman was one of the best singers I had ever heard! Her voice and spirit seemed to ignite the rest of the congregation each time she led out in song. One thing was certain: no one was distracted by the band or anything else onstage (something that can be a problem in churches in the U.S.). These folks were there to praise the Lord!

I finally found the leader. Sitting in the section to the right of the center aisle, about five rows from the front, was a young woman who looked to be about fifteen or sixteen years old. Her hands were raised, her head was lifted up, and she had a glorious glow on her face. She knew where the holy place was and how to get there, and everyone followed her in! This was worship leading in its purest form.

I began to have a great time. When the songs were in English, I sang as I learned how the songs went. When they were in the native languages, I sang in tongues. It was really good. There was such a freedom without any performance or ego trips going on that it freed us all up to focus completely on Jesus.

I returned home having learned that we don't have to change our stage setup or only have one keyboard on stage. I don't have to sit in the fifth row or get rid of the rest of the band. But no matter what logistical structure we have, it should be what the Holy Spirit has shown us is best for who we are. And whatever it is, we must totally abandon ourselves to worshiping and praising our Savior.

From that time on, we began to experience a new freedom and release to the Lord, and He in turn poured out His love like never before. I had learned a first-class lesson from what some call "third-world" people. Love God, believe His word, and praise Him with all of your heart.

Kirk and Deby Dearman

Few songwriters reach the pinnacle of praise-and-worship recognition that Kirk and Deby Dearman achieved in one song. "We Bring the Sacrifice of Praise" has been sung in virtually every language and was

listed for ten years in Christian Copyright Licensing International's top ten songs sung by the church universally.

Kirk and Deby have traveled extensively throughout North America, Great Britain, and continental Europe and presently live in Nashville, Tennessee, where they lead worship, write songs, and record.

In addition to leading worship in churches and at conferences, the Dearmans tour with a worship service called Come to the Quiet, a multisensory encounter with God designed to quiet and refresh the soul. Created by Kirk and Deby to help the church-present connect with the church-past, Come to the Quiet features brilliant imagery, moving songs, and inspiring meditations.

Kirk and Deby send out a monthly e-newsletter, "Internet Retreat for the Soul," a collection of devotions, photographs, and free song downloads, available through their website, www.cometothequiet.com.

MAKE HIS PRAISE GLORIOUS
by Kirk and Deby Dearman

In 1984 our family moved to Europe. We joined long-time friends Jim and Anne Mills in the ancient city of Augsburg, Germany. Many weeks were given to prayer and worship as we listened together for the voice of God to clarify our call. Our mission as songwriters and worship leaders became clear: we were to make His praise glorious (Psalm 66:2). The overall title of our ministry became "Demonstrating Praise to the Nations," and our touring company was called "Project Exalt!"

While meditating on the scripture "make His praise glorious," our spirits began to soar as we envisioned creative worship services incorporating the arts. We pictured candlelight processions, worshipers bowing at the altars of beautiful cathedrals, dancers kneeling in prayer and lying prostrate before the cross—true expressions of lives yielded to the Savior. We longed to share not only through song lyrics but also through actual worshipers expressing through movement what the lyrics proclaimed.

We quickly found that our frustrations in verbally sharing the gospel were overcome by adding the visual arts to worship. Our praise enhanced by visual expression seemed to bypass the intellect and go straight to the heart. Worship music and sacred dance choreographed together as an expression of our faith became our new method of ministry. Hopes and dreams of leading Europeans into the presence of God were realized in the form of a worship musical titled *Canticum ad Deum*, Latin for "Song Unto God."

We enlisted an international team of musicians and dancers, all of whom were young Christians excited about using their gifts and talents for the Lord. We wrote songs and translated them into German. After an intensive training time, we began our tour throughout Europe.

Looking back on our ministry in Europe, we realize that the arts, when combined with worship, are more powerful than we had ever imagined. Hard hearts melted and stone faces softened as dancers beautifully expressed their hearts and exalted Jesus. With graceful movements, trained dancers bypassed language and intellectual barriers. The art form itself spoke volumes!

Visual images became sermons we could never find words to express. The songs were simple and led the way into the holy of holies. Our audience sensed the tangible presence of God, many for the first time in their lives.

Symbol played an important role in our worship experience as well. Magnificent cathedrals provided a sacred space already dedicated to the glory of God. Complete with brilliant stained-glass windows, intricate mosaics, and inspiring frescos, the very ground we stood on reflected God's glory. The bread, cup, Bible, cross, and candles carried down the aisle in procession prepared the audience for the message. The people were desperate for hope and a faith they could see, touch, and feel. Not only did they hear, but also they vividly saw the message. Now they had sacred symbols from which to draw inspiration to enter into God's presence themselves.

Project Exalt! continued for several years as we ministered in cathedrals with worship teams. The ministry, now called Creative Arts Europe, is still flourishing. Led by Jim and Anne Mills, it is based at The Arts House in Brussels, Belgium.

As we returned to the States in 1991, we began to experience a void in corporate worship. In the midst of culture shock and reentry, we would go to church desperately needing time to sit quietly in God's presence and be washed from the stress and strain of life. Often we would go home disappointed. It seemed that too many worship times were loud, hyped, or sometimes cut short if a silent moment occurred. Something deep within us yearned for time to linger in the Lord's presence. We needed time to heal from the storms that so often surrounded us.

When we were invited to start a monthly worship service at St. Matthias Episcopal Church in Nashville, Tennessee, we realized that God was giving us the opportunity to birth a different kind of worship service that might meet the needs we were feeling. As we waited in listening prayer, God spoke and the vision became clear—a service of worship incorporating the arts! We decided to name this service "Come to the Quiet." We began to build on the foundation that had been laid in the cathedrals of Europe.

Symbol had become so important to us. We longed to once again experience the beauty of symbol we had found in the cathedrals. As we allowed God to shape our vision, we felt that He wanted us to incorporate the use of candlelight, ringing bells, interpretive reading of Scripture, processions, music, and responsive readings around a particular theme. Sensing that the church was longing to reconnect with its historical roots, we began to study church history and set various ancient creeds and prayers to music.

As worship leaders now at Christ Episcopal Church in Mobile, Alabama, we have introduced "Come to the Quiet" as a regular ministry. It has been so exciting to see the artists of our church come alive as their gifts are utilized in worship: visual arts people, carpenters, painters, songwriters, script writers, readers, sound and light technicians, musicians, actors, dancers—all worshiping the Lord with their gifts. Our church now sees this service as an outreach to the community, as it draws many who would never come to a typical Sunday service.

As we move into the twenty-first century, our methods of communicating the gospel must be relevant to the times and to our culture. We live in a visually oriented society, and we are daily bombarded with ungodly symbols and imagery. We believe that God wants to restore symbol and imagery to His church.

As worship leaders, each of us has a unique call. It is vital that we spend time in the Lord's presence listening before we lead. His ideas are so far above anything we could create on our own. If we don't listen, how will we discover the unique way He has called us to present His Word and lead people into His presence?

Lynn DeShazo

 Lynn DeShazo is a gifted worship leader and the writer of numerous songs, many of which have appeared on Integrity's Hosanna! Music recordings. Lynn is presently an exclusive songwriter for Integrity Music and is best known for such songs as "More Precious Than Silver," "Lead Me to the Rock," "You Have Called Us," "Turn My Heart," and "Be Magnified."

Lynn resides in her hometown, Birmingham, Alabama. When she is not on the road as part of her traveling ministry, she serves as worship leader and musician at Liberty Church.

My Pastor, My Encourager

by Lynn DeShazo

I remember very distinctly the day my pastor asked me to take over the worship-leading responsibilities for our small fellowship in Ann Arbor, Michigan. The request came as a surprise to me, even though I had been a part of our worship team since the inception of the church three years earlier. Our current worship leader, an excellent musician, would soon be leaving, and the "mantle" was being passed to me.

I replied, "Well ... okay, Mike, but I'd be happy just to play guitar while you lead, if you'd rather do it that way." Interpretation: "I'm not so sure about this. Wouldn't you like to be a worship-leading pastor?"

The truth was, I probably would have been quite content just playing along with the worship team, at least for a while. I was quite comfortable in the familiar role of a supporting (i.e., not in charge) team member.

Pastor Mike Caulk, however, was undaunted by my hesitance. "Lynn, you have an anointing on your life to lead worship. I know you can do this!" He assured me that I was suited for the task and that we would work together as a team until the transition was successfully made. Pastor Mike and I put our heads together on song lists for worship services and practiced with the rest of the worship team on Saturdays. On Sunday mornings Mike would call the congregation to worship and lead us in heartily sung praise medleys, often interspersed with exhortations. I'd play along, leading the other musicians and helping us all to make the transitions between songs.

We hit our share of snags, of course. Sometimes Mike's exhortations turned into minisermons, and we'd lose the flow. Sometimes I'd miss his cues to go on to the next song, and we'd sound like a train wreck. Occasionally Mike would lean over and whisper, "How do we end this song?" and I'd try to keep from breaking up in laughter.

All in all, our approach worked out pretty well. The Lord was praised, we had fun, and my confidence grew. The day eventually came when Mike stepped down from his interim role as worship leader and turned that responsibility completely over to me.

A true pastor wants to see each of the sheep entrusted to his care grow into a mature believer. He recognizes that God never intended him to do everything himself (even when it seems easier that way) but intended him to train and disciple the church to do the work of ministry with increasing effectiveness.

Perhaps the most important feat accomplished in that transitional period was the growth of my confidence. My pastor prodded me in a direction that I needed to step out in and then wisely gave me all the practical support he was capable of until I could lead a worship service on my own. I don't remember that day as clearly as the other one, but I must have done all right, because I kept the job for the next five years. Leading God's people in worship continues to be a prime area of ministry for me.

Brian Doerksen

Brian Doerksen is a first-generation Canadian, born in British Columbia and brought up in the Mennonite Brethren Church. As a teenager he began to experience a strong anointing as a songwriter and worship leader. After high school he attended a training school with Youth With A Mission and later moved to Langley, B.C., to work with the Langley Vineyard Christian Fellowship.

In the late 1990s Brian lived for two years in the UK, where he trained worship leaders and songwriters in the UK and Ireland and produced two popular worship albums, Hungry and Come, Now Is the Time. After returning to live in Canada, he continued to produce for Vineyard Music and then recorded his first project with Integrity, You Shine, in 2002. His latest recording with Integrity, called Today, was released in 2004 and was the number-two selling Christian CD in Canada for 2004 and the winner of numerous awards.

Brian's songs include "Come, Now Is the Time to Worship," which has appeared in the top three on the CCLI charts, "Hope of the Nations," "Faithful One," "Refiner's Fire," and "Hallelujah (Your Love Is Amazing)."

Currently Brian is developing a musical of hope based on Luke 15 called Return and is preparing for his third recording with Integrity.

He and his wife of of twenty-one years, Joyce, live in Abbotsford, B.C., with their six children.

BREAKING THE FEAR OF MAN
by Brian Doerksen

~✦ **W**orship is all about people noticing God, not us. To be effective worship leaders, we must give up the desire to impress people and have them notice us. Because of this, the Lord will sometimes ask us to do things to see whether we fear Him more than the people before whom we are standing.

I vividly remember this happening to me. In fact I think it was the very first time I led worship for the conservative evangelical church I grew up in. They had asked me to lead worship for the Sunday-night youth service. That night everything started out fine. Then the still small voice whispered to me, "Kneel down and worship Me." Inside I argued, "They *never* do that here. What will people think of me?" It came again with more force: "Kneel down." I recognized that God was trying to break the fear of man in me. Finally I obeyed, and I felt a sweet release. I no longer led by singing and exhortation but led by example, and this has been a key for me ever since. My desire is to build up the body through worship. I have found that I ultimately do the best job of this when I'm totally obedient to the Head of the church—Jesus.

THE HEALING PRESENCE OF GOD IN INSTRUMENTAL MUSIC
by Brian Doerksen

~✦ **M**usic is a wonderful thing. It is something that God created to move all of who we are. Sometimes no words are needed. In fact, sometimes words can even trivialize or cheapen the communication. This has been illustrated to me powerfully more than once. In the summer of 1992 we hosted the "Worship Festival" here in Langley, with Graham Kendrick, Bob Fitts, and other worship leaders from the Vineyard. During the very last session, I was leading worship and felt like the Lord had said to recommit our vows to Him. As we neared the end, we began an instrumental piece I had written called "Rest in Me." After this song we planned to go into "Song for the Bride." As we began, I sensed I should call my wife onto the stage with me and that I should hold her while the music played as a picture of the intimacy that Jesus, the groom, wants to have with His bride. Not a word was spoken, but the truth and emotion of God's love was powerfully communicated through the simple music and act. Many people cried and sensed the nearness of the presence of God.

Another time, I was leading worship for the evening service at the Anaheim Vineyard while I was in town doing a recording. As many people came to the front for ministry at the close of the service, I had an impression that many of these people had wounds. God wanted us to play healing notes over them. I turned to my electric guitar player Brian Thiessen and briefly explained what I sensed. Brian then began to play notes— long, sustained notes. Sometimes he would repeat a note or he would play a different note. Amazingly, I observed that different notes had different effects on different people. Later I talked with several people who said that whenever a certain note was played, they felt a "healing presence" enter them.

Music is a powerful tool in the hands of God to bring life and healing. I believe more and more that we will see what David saw when he played for King Saul. As worship leaders, we should sometimes be careful not to fill the air with so many words so that the music can do its healing work.

SIMPLICITY, BROKENNESS, AND AN OUT-OF-TUNE PIANO

by Brian Doerksen

It was another hot day. The air was so thick our clothes stuck to our bodies. We were riding on the back of a tap-tap, the common public transportation in Haiti, where I had come for a short-term mission experience. After several hours we reached our destination, a town in the center of Haiti. Days like this make you ask questions like, "What am I doing here? Did God really call me to come on this trip?"

We had not been able to make previous arrangements as to where we would stay, but a missionary family graciously let us stay with them. By this time it had been quite a while since we had had a time of worship together. We understood that instruments were quite rare in Haiti, but they told us they had a piano in the chapel. We went right away so that we could have a long-awaited time of worship and refreshment. I sat down at the piano and started to play. The piano was completely out of tune. I mean totally!

I immediately sensed the Lord speaking. "Will you worship Me anyway, even with the out-of-tune piano?" I found one octave with relatively in-tune bass notes, began playing one note at a time and singing. Immediately the presence of God was evident, and my tears began to flow. It was one of the sweetest times of worship I've ever had.

The truth is, I guess we are a lot like that out-of-tune piano. Yet God is still able to play His melody of love on our lives despite our weaknesses and failures.

In the middle of the push for excellence in worship music (which I wholeheartedly endorse), I'll never forget that sometimes the most powerful things come through broken people and whatever we have. God's not waiting for us to get our act together so He can use us. He's waiting for our brokenness and humility.

Eddie Espinosa

Eddie Espinosa was born in Los Angeles, California, and was raised in the Catholic church, where he served as an altar boy. In 1969, at the age of fifteen, Eddie gave his heart to Jesus Christ in a deeper way. On the following day he was taken to a youth rally, where he saw Andraé Crouch leading people into the presence of God. Eddie immediately knew he was called to do the same.

Although he is a pastor, Eddie is most widely known as a worship leader and songwriter. He has composed such popular songs as "You Are the Mighty King," "Most of All," and "Change My Heart, O God." His heart's desire is to see Psalm 67 come to pass: "May the peoples praise You, O God; may all the peoples praise You."

Eddie's passion for the Lord is evident in his music and worship leading. He has been a worship leader at the Vineyard in Anaheim for over twelve years.

Eddie and his wife, Elsie, have two children and reside in Anaheim, California.

To Make a List or Not Make a List? That Is the Question!

by Eddie Espinosa

One day one of the members of the worship team said to me that he thought that the worship was flat and dull because I was using a prepared list of songs. Because I respect the people who are a part of our music ministry, I took his comment very seriously. I even prayed about it. "O God, if the way I'm planning or even the fact that I am planning is getting in the way of what You want to do in our worship, I ask You to correct me, to teach me, even to rebuke me if necessary." I continued on and told the Lord that I did not want to be a hindrance to what He was wanting to do.

At the end of my prayer time I made a deal with the Lord. I said, "Lord, I would like to do a little experiment. I'm going to pray and prepare just as I normally do when I lead worship. I'm even going to make a list, just as usual. But I'm not going to give that list to the worship team. And one more thing, Lord. I'd like permission, just this once, to disobey You." What I meant by that last statement was that if during the worship set I felt led to deviate from my prepared list and do a different song spontaneously, I would continue to go by the list. As I prayed I felt like this was all acceptable to the Lord.

On the given Sunday morning, the worship team prayed and went over a few songs, but I didn't let anybody see my list. I kept it hidden. Nobody knew I even had a list. As I was leading worship, I kept going down the list that I had made, exactly as I had written it.

Worship went really well. It went so well, in fact, that the same team member who had confronted me came up to me after worship and said, "Eddie, worship was fantastic! It was so great. I just can't believe it was so good!" He continued, "I betcha I know why, too. It's 'cause you got rid of the stinkin' list."

"Well," I responded, "actually I took what you said very seriously." Then I told him the whole process that I had gone through. I finished by explaining, "As a matter of fact I did go by the list, and I did the songs in the exact same order." The look on his face was great. I wish I had had a camera.

As a worship leader, I always try to find the best way to lead worship. One of the things that I have found to be important is to seek the Lord beforehand and to prepare myself by making a song list. I see leading worship very much like preparing a sermon. A good pastor prepares carefully ahead of time, putting much time and prayer into a sermon. Without this preparation he is, in essence, saying that he is unwilling to put the necessary time into prayer, meditation, and listening to the Lord.

Jesus said that He did only what He saw the Father doing. Moses followed the pillar of cloud and the pillar of fire and moved only when they moved. In the same way we as worship leaders need to be followers of the Holy Spirit. He is really the worship leader. We are simply following what He wants to emphasize when we lead.

The issue is not whether or not to make a list. The issue is that if you make a list, make it according to what you believe the Holy Spirit is telling you for that particular service. I believe we need to prepare and plan and yet be flexible and leave room for the nudging of the Holy Spirit to lead us in another direction during the service.

What I do is pray during the week and ask the Lord to bring songs to my mind. Then I write them down. I also ask the person who will be giving the message what topic and/or particular Scripture he or she will be speaking on. Oftentimes the Lord will give me songs that go along with the topic without my even knowing what that topic is. I believe we need to be flexible and to plan according to what the Lord is saying.

THE "G" FACTOR
by Eddie Espinosa

There was a pastors' conference going on, and I was leading worship. About two thousand pastors and leaders were in attendance. Halfway through the worship set the Lord told me to "go into repentance songs."

I remember arguing with the Lord and saying, "Lord, this is a pastors' conference, and all these guys are leaders and pastors. They're right on with You." Then, very distinctly, He once again said, "Repentance songs." I finally conceded to what I was certain God was saying. I began to sing Psalm 51, "Create in Me a Clean Heart," "Change My Heart, O God," "It's Your Blood That Cleanses Me," and another series of songs about repentance and forgiveness and the blood of Christ.

After that, we went into some more songs about intimacy with God, drawing close to Him, and the Father loving us. I assumed that there would be a word of prophecy or encouragement given that had to do with repentance. Nothing happened! I thought, *Well maybe the message is on repentance and our need to be before God.* Still nothing happened. Then I thought maybe somebody was going to sing a special number. Still nothing. By this time I was feeling very defeated, certain that I had completely missed God.

Finally about forty-five minutes after I had finished leading worship, the pastor who was in charge of the meeting looked at the congregation and said, "I really feel that someone here has a word from the Lord for us." A brother in the back row raised his hand, stood up, and said, "I feel that there are people here who have seen their ministry and are performing their ministry as though they are hirelings and not as shepherds." That simple statement broke the hearts of a lot of pastors and leaders. As a result, about three hundred pastors and leaders came up to the altar, weeping and repenting. It was a wonderful time when God was meeting people's needs.

To me the question was, Did I cause that to happen as a worship leader? No! I believe that there are two things a worship leader cannot take for himself, and they both begin with the letter G. The first is *glory* when things go well, and the second is *guilt* when things don't go quite as planned. I did not cause the time of ministry to happen. God was going to do what He wanted to do with or without me. But it was such a blessing for me to take part in what God was doing. It was a perfect example for me of doing what the Father wanted instead of what my own rational judgment thought was appropriate at the time. In following the direction of the Lord, we need obedience and flexibility.

Darrell Evans

Darrell Evans began his walk with Christ when he was only eleven years old. Shortly thereafter, he began writing songs and leading other youth in worship. Eventually, following evangelism and ministry

training, Darrell served as youth pastor and worship leader for churches in California, Washington, and Oklahoma.

Darrell's albums include Hosanna! Music recording Let the River Flow *and Vertical Music recordings* You Are I Am *and* Freedom. *His songs include "Let the River Flow," "We Will Embrace (Your Move)," and "My God Reigns."*

When Darrell was a kid he wanted to be a comedian. In fact, he does a pretty impressive Jerry Lewis impersonation.

Darrell and his wife, Gayla, reside in Mobile, Alabama. From Mobile they head River Flow Ministries, a full-time worship-concert ministry that is carrying them into churches across the U.S.

THE PLAYGROUND OF PRAISE

by Darrell Evans

ne of my favorite things to do is to take long walks and spend time in worship and prayer. Some of the most significant exchanges between the Lord and me occur while I am on these walks. Sometimes I listen to a worship tape on my Walkman, sometimes I simply walk and talk with the Lord, and some days I just quiet my heart and listen. Often worship songs are birthed out of these prayer walks.

About three years ago I was out on a walk with the Lord through my neighborhood heading toward a nearby elementary schoolyard. As I approached a football field, I was listening to a demo recording of a new song that I was writing: "We'll dance and we'll sing, for our God is the Ancient of Days." I felt the Father tugging at my heart, saying, "I want you to dance for Me. I want you to dance with Me." I stopped the tape. Still, I kept hearing, "Will you dance for Me?" It was as though the Holy Spirit was saying, "You said you would in the song. Now will you dance for me out here on this field?"

At this point in my life I had been a worship leader for several years. Although I believed that dancing before the Lord was a biblical expression of praise, it was not an expression in which I felt freedom. I particularly enjoyed the quiet love songs and intimate times with the Lord. Anytime in my life when there had been an opportunity to dance before the Lord, I usually felt as though the worship leader was trying to hype it up or manipulate me into that expression. The truth is that I simply used that as an excuse.

So here the Lord was, asking me to go for it out on a football field. On one side was a line of neighborhood houses with their backyards facing me, and on the other side was the school playground where the kids were playing at recess. I had an opportunity to let the Lord release in me a childlike heart of worship.

After a few moments of indecision I turned the music on again. I thought, "Okay, here we go." I started at one end of the field and began dancing and spinning my way toward the other end. About halfway down the field, I began shouting (another valid biblical expression of worship that was always difficult for me) at the top of my lungs, "Hey, hey, hey, freedom!" Over and over again I yelled and spun around and danced before the Lord. It was great! I didn't care who might see or hear me.

I had known the reverence of an awesome God and the intimacy of a loving Jesus. However, at that moment I was truly understanding the joy of a totally abandoned childlike heart. I was celebrating with my Father on this football field that I was His son. Something in me had cracked and peeled. A layer of pride had been pulled away. I had a new sense of freedom. This freedom translated into leading others into the same abandonment in worship.

I believe that our personalities can affect our interaction with the Lord. However, this should never be used as an excuse to give God anything less than what Scripture calls for as passionate and creative expressions of worship to the Lord. "That's not my personality" doesn't work with the Lord. The very nature of worship is to step beyond ourselves and recognize that He is greater and we are less. He is our Father and we are His kids.

Is there one thing that you said you would never do in worship? Is there one expression you could never see yourself helping others experience? Do that! The result will be new levels of freedom in your life and in the lives of those you humbly intend to serve.

Bob Fitts

To bring healing to the nations with the message of hope and encouragement in Jesus is the focus of the ministry of Bob Fitts. Bob has trav-

eled to many parts of the world, teaching, singing, and worshiping with groups of people across denominational and cultural boundaries, drawing them deeper into love relationships with the Father.

Bob is a well-known songwriter and recording artist. He is the featured singer and worship leader on four of Integrity's Hosanna! Music albums, The Lord Reigns, Highest Place, Bethlehem's Treasure, *and* Proclaim His Power. *He is also featured on Maranatha! Music's* Live Worship with Bob Fitts *and on two solo albums with Scripture and Song's Earth Mover division,* Take My Healing to the Nations *and* Sacrifice.

The many songs Bob has written include "Blessed Be the Lord God Almighty," "He Is Lovely," and "Let It Rain."

Since 1981 Bob has worked with Youth With A Mission in Kailua-Kona, Hawaii, where he pioneered the School of Worship at YWAM's University of the Nations. Bob and his wife, Kathy, and their four children reside in Kailua-Kona, Hawaii.

WHEN LIFE HAPPENS, LIVE IT
by Bob Fitts

If there is one message that is difficult to teach regarding worship, it is the message of *flexibility* and *humility*. Anyone involved in worship leading, or any public ministry for that matter, knows the challenge of developing these two very important character traits. Because heart issues are much more difficult to deal with than just passing on information, teaching them is often put on the back burner and replaced with some good, strong head knowledge. It makes us feel better! We can then take an exam, be graded, and have a form of evaluation put on ourselves and others. That would seem to be an all right thing to do—except that life comes along and happens! My wife and I have developed a saying: *When life happens, live it.*

I remember a few years ago when a young boy attending the youth ministry that I was leading wanted me to take him on a roller coaster ride. All of our group had traveled together to an amusement park (which specialized in roller coasters), and there we were, standing with our mouths wide open, looking up at this monster of a thrill ride. This young boy, whom I will call Bobby, kept saying, "Take me on it! Take me on it!" So after not too much persuasion, I got in line with Bobby and proceeded to enter the ride.

Now for those of you who have ridden roller coasters (however you feel about them), you realize that the moment you strap in, life begins to happen, and a funny thing goes on in your stomach (kind of the same feeling you get just before you lead worship for the first time). It is a mixture of fear and antic-ipation that, for some, is what the joy of living is all about—just enough challenge or danger to make your heart start pumping, and just enough safety so that you know nothing is really dangerous about it at all. It's almost an exercise in tor-ture, isn't it? Thrill rides are an effort to fool our senses into believing that we are really in danger. Sometimes our bodies (at least mine) take the bait. We are really scared!

As Bobby and I embarked up that long hill, chain clicking, the sky looming before us as though we were heading straight into the clouds, Bobby looked at me with the most horrified, pale little face and said, "I want to get off!" Oh, I'm just sure! As we went over the edge, my leadership skills went into high gear. "Yo-o, ain't this fun!" I said in a desperate attempt to sal-vage Bobby's confidence. (Worship leaders, pay attention: there are lots of parallels to note here!) No response, not even breathing, just terror. That hill finished, Bobby took a breath and with all his might screamed, "Get me off of this!"

How many times we've all felt like running offstage and dying. Just when you think it could never be worse—just ahead looms the next hill, more terror. By this time I was pretty upset that I had done such a stupid thing. However, by now the ride was almost over and things actually started to get fun. Bobby was gaining color and beginning to scream for joy. And then it began to happen, both my and Bobby's perspective of the ride began to change. Thoughts like "Boy, wait till I tell my friends about this ride" and "I meant to do that" were racing through our minds. After disembarking, little Bobby was right at me, wanting to get on again! Ha! I was amazed. What seemed to be total disaster and danger a few minutes earlier had now become one of the most memorable moments of my life (as is obvious by this very printing).

What did I learn? When life happens, live it. Hang on, my friend. What seems to be disaster is really all under control. You might say, "What on earth does this have to do with worship leading?" If you have done much leading or planning of meetings, you should quickly catch the parallels. Leading God's people to the place of praise and worship is one aspect of leadership that will always present an opportunity for real life to happen. How flexible and faithful we are in those situations determines not only how well people relate to us but also how much all of us will enjoy experiencing the thrill of serving and honoring the Lord Jesus in praise and worship.

The second of these two very important characteristics (and the one more obviously referred to in Scripture)—humility—is one I will relate in this next story. I remember once being asked to lead worship for a very large gathering of people. The praise team I was working with were incredible singers and musicians, most of them gifted worship leaders in their own right. As we were diligently rehearsing one day, I overheard one of the musicians comment about a young man who had written a song and wanted to present it in front of all these thousands of people. We were all a bit bothered by this, getting quite arrogant in exchanging different horror stories of people who had felt they needed to sing a song and were not ready for it (at least in our estimation). I could feel a bit of pride creeping into our rehearsal, and the Holy Spirit whispered to me, "Be careful." As I have led worship all over the world, I have come to recognize that voice as God's way of saying, "Don't put too much trust in your skill, in your gifting and talent. Trust Me!" I told the team that God would probably humble us all and powerfully use the song.

Sure enough, that young boy was asked to get up in front of the conference and tell about a revival taking place on his high-school campus. After giving his testimony he stood in great fear and trembling—but with a heart of humility and a desire to honor God—and sang the song of praise that the Holy Spirit had given him. He sang not so excellently, and the song (by songwriter criteria) was not so good, but God's Spirit loved the humble heart of His young servant and graced that auditorium with His wonderful presence. Here we were, these wonderful, educated, gifted people with loads of experience and knowledge to put our trust in, and God chose the young, humble servant whose confidence was not in his gift but in his God!

Passing along to others the traits of flexibility and humility is not an easy task. Teaching life is difficult. We must do so by living it to its fullest. The Scriptures say, "Knowledge puffs up" (1 Corinthians 8:1). It's not often that we major on that concept in our schools of worship! I mean, aren't we there to teach people how to sing and play instruments and be good leaders? Doesn't God want us to have schools to teach people and to give them knowledge? Yes, but we also need a different kind of knowledge, the knowledge that God's ways are not our ways. We must learn the ways that get us outside our safe, neat little environment and get us away from a rigid style that says, "If you lead this song, they'll do that; if you say this phrase, this will happen; if you sing . . . " and so on. Certainly structure is important and a key component of any roller coaster. But in the analogy, getting on the ride means turning ultimate control over to the designer of the ride. Letting the Creator of life teach us through life's unexpected situations is sometimes the more difficult way of leading. Teaching structure is relatively easy; teaching lifestyle means we have to live it ourselves, walk it ourselves, "ride it" ourselves, even in front of those we lead.

Every praise service is God's moment to design a "new ride." As I have observed in retrospect just how much fun I get out of thinking about these kinds of situations, I find myself enjoying building roller coasters with tracks that go straight up the wall in seemingly disastrous configurations. God is not like that! He is good! He is the Author of abundant life!

Rick Founds

Rick Founds has been leading worship since he was fourteen years old. He has written numerous songs that are used every week in church services worldwide. His songs include "Lord, I Lift Your Name on High," "Jesus, Mighty God," "I Need You," and "Jesus, Draw Me Close."

Rick's educational and career activities are diverse and include studies in music therapy, accounting, welding, and machine sciences. He has a degree in radio media technology and has experience in research-and-development engineering in the fiber optics illumination industry. With over twelve years of full-time music ministry experience, Rick has recently been involved in a new church plant called The Comfort Zone Ministries.

Rick lives in Southern California with his wife, three children, two cats, and three fish (used to be four fish, but that's another story).

GRUESOME WORSHIP

by Rick Founds

There was blood all over the guy's face. It was like something out of a *Friday the 13th* movie.

It was a hot, sweaty Thursday evening, smack in the middle of one of the warmest summers on record. The sanctuary was filled to capacity, and the air conditioning wasn't working all that well. This was one of those periodic special nights of worship. We would exchange the normal time allotted for in-depth study with an extended time of praise, worship, and prayer.

The Spirit of God was present in a very powerful way, despite the muggy conditions. Throughout the building, people were enthusiastically singing and worshiping the Lord. Most people had their eyes closed, some with hands raised, some standing in awe, some sitting, some quietly kneeling, as the worship team continued to lead with songs of gratitude and love to our Lord and Savior.

For the past few songs I had been singing with my eyes closed, enjoying a particularly clear sense of the love and presence of Jesus. I became aware of a sound behind me and slightly to my right. Turning my head in that direction, I opened my eyes. There was my drummer, head down, still quietly and sensitively keeping the beat, but his shoulders were trembling.

Wow, I thought. *He is really in tune with the presence of God tonight. There he is, gently weeping as he worships God with skillful praise.*

Then he looked up. He stared at me with pain in his eyes—the pain that only comes with trying to suppress extremely inappropriate laughter. He glanced toward the front row, just to my left. I followed his gaze.

The poor guy in the front row looked like he had just been pulled from a severe car accident! Blood in his hair. Blood smeared all over his forehead, cheeks, and chin. Blood on what was once a nice blue shirt. Blood on one of the hands he had raised to the heavens.

Oh no! I thought to myself. *We've got one of those wacko cult weirdos. One of these people, like the ancient prophets of Baal, who thinks he needs to mutilate himself in order to be heard by God.* Great. Now what? My drummer had nearly bitten off his own tongue to keep from laughing, but he kept on playing. Miraculously, nobody else seemed to have noticed yet. I thought to myself, *Better do another sing-to-the-Lord-with-your-eyes-closed type of song till I can get some help here.*

Finally I began to understand what was happening. It was hot. It was sweaty. This guy had some kind of scab on his neck. Maybe from a cut or scrape. Maybe it was a giant zit. I don't know, but there it was. It had been itching, and he'd been scratching. It was a morbidly fascinating thing to watch. I observed with great wonder as I continued to sing the melody and lyric of the current song. (An interesting experience, kind of like juggling with your brain.) There he sat, with eyes closed and hands lifted. From all indications his heart was comfortably situated before the throne of God. What he was completely unaware of was the fact that as he would unconsciously respond to the itch on his neck, he would uncoagulate his wound, collect a fresh supply of blood on his palm and fingers, and rub his hand across his face, through his hair, and finally across the front of his shirt. Then he would reverently lift his hand once again in honor to the God of heaven.

I was able to get the attention of one of the other singers onstage. I indicated with my head in the direction of the activity in the front row. She read my mind and quietly slipped offstage and quickly made her way to the nearby kitchen area. She returned in a flash with a moistened dish towel and managed to graciously make the gentleman aware of his situation. The man's face took on that priceless expression of perplexed shock as he opened his eyes to the sight of his own bloody hand. Fortunately, he had the presence of mind not to scream. He thankfully accepted the damp towel and quietly disappeared. Shortly thereafter he slipped back into the sanctuary. His face was scrubbed clean, and he wore a lightweight windbreaker over his stained shirt and a large bandage on his neck. Our friend resumed worship as if nothing had happened.

"Let's all stand and sing," I said. "Open our eyes, Lord; we want to see Jesus."

Steve Fry

Steve Fry is the president of Messenger Fellowship, a community of leaders who have a passion for being rooted in both the lordship of Jesus Christ and the power of the Spirit and who come together for

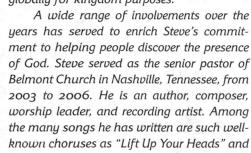

strategic ministry, partnering locally and globally for kingdom purposes.

A wide range of involvements over the years has served to enrich Steve's commitment to helping people discover the presence of God. Steve served as the senior pastor of Belmont Church in Nashville, Tennessee, from 2003 to 2006. He is an author, composer, worship leader, and recording artist. Among the many songs he has written are such well-known choruses as "Lift Up Your Heads" and "Oh the Glory of Your Presence." Steve has also penned two widely acclaimed musicals, We Are Called *and* Thy Kingdom Come.

Steve and his wife, Nancy, and their three children live in Brentwood, Tennessee.

GOD INHABITS OUR PRAISES

by Steve Fry

~~ For a number of years I had the privilege of leading high-school and college students in various outreaches around the world. On one occasion I was coordinating a group of about two hundred young people in a street witnessing campaign in downtown Washington, D.C. We had chosen a park in an area of the city that we later found out was one of the most violent in the entire District. So violent was this particular neighborhood that drivers could not stop their cars and most certainly could not drive with unlocked doors for fear that their car doors would be ripped open and they'd be robbed at knifepoint.

When we arrived at this particular park, we were confronted with a kaleidoscope of sights and sounds—pimps, prostitutes, and pushers, streetwise waifs, and world-weary panhandlers. As we began to fan out through the park and surrounding neighborhoods, sharing Christ's love with people, we soon realized that we were encountering forces of spiritual darkness that were beyond what we had encountered in the past. The atmosphere itself seemed to be charged with violence; some were becoming so belligerent that they accosted us within six inches of our faces, screaming obscenities. We knew that the situation could rapidly escalate beyond our control, so we got some of the musicians together and began to play and sing praises to Jesus. Over the next several minutes we witnessed nothing short of a miraculous transformation. Suddenly a sense of peace and calm descended over the park. Where onlookers were before seething in their hatred, we now saw high-school students sitting down and chatting amiably with scores of men and women about their eternal destiny. Later we found out that in the ensuing hour, twelve people gave their hearts to Christ!

What had made the difference? The difference was that the *authority of Jesus was brought to bear on that park through the praise and worship of His people.* Psalm 22:3 says that the Lord inhabits the praises of His people. A better translation is that the authority of the Lord is experientially realized in the context of praise. In other words, praise makes room for the kingdom of Jesus to be established in a particular situation at a particular time. Never had Psalm 22:3 been made so real to me than on that day when I witnessed a bastion of violence transformed into an oasis of peace.

HEAVEN ON EARTH
by Steve Fry

Paul, the apostle, says in Ephesians 2:6 that we are seated with Christ in heavenly places. Paul's statement can be taken several ways. Is this a descriptive foretaste of what is to come? Is it Paul's way of poetically expressing our authority in Christ? Or does Paul's statement actually comment on present reality? After all, Paul is couching his words in the present tense. He says we are situated in a certain way at this very moment. We "are seated"—present tense—"in heavenly places in Christ Jesus."

How can this bear on a present reality that finds us fighting traffic jams and balancing checkbooks? Actually there is something extraordinarily potent contained in this passage that, when we get a handle on it, will revolutionize our perspective and thus transform our lives.

The truth of this text was brought home forcefully to me some years ago when I was leading a group of college students in worship. We experienced an extraordinary encounter with the presence of God, and afterwards a college student, whom I had noticed sitting in the back row, came up to me with eyes as big as his face, his mouth gaping in awe. Knowing something of this young man's background, I knew that he was an avid basketball player, and he had his Reeboks firmly planted on the gymnasium floor. He was not one given to mystical visions. Yet here he was staring at me in semidisbelief, describing to me what he had just seen while we were worshiping.

"While you were leading us in worship," he began recounting to me, "I saw two angelic beings on either side of you, so tall that I could not see beyond their shoulders. I looked straight up, and as far as my eyes could see, I could still catch no more than their upper body. But the incredible thing was that behind you I saw the very feet of God." Now his encounter shouldn't surprise us, because Scripture records in Exodus 24 that the elders under Moses also saw the feet of God from within the cloud of glory on Sinai. Had this young man seen a vision? I don't think so. I think for just a moment his eyes were opened to see where we actually live—in heavenly places!

You see, we're so used to thinking of heaven in directional terms, that it is a realm beyond the universe. But heaven is not so much to be understood in directional terms—up, down, right, or left—but in *dimensional terms*. Heaven is not another direction but another dimension, coexisting quite literally with the material world. So in a very real sense, we are living in heaven now!

"If that's true, it sure doesn't feel like heaven down here," someone might say. That is only because our perspective has not been altered. We are citizens of heaven, expressing that life in the earthly realm. Though our eyes cannot see it, we are quite literally living in heavenly places now in Christ Jesus!

Yet someone might question, "What does this have to do with worship?" Everything! For if I realize that heaven is a dimension coexisting with the material world, then when I enter into worship, I am actually joining the procession of the angelic hosts in lauding and adoring God. I am not attempting to coax God to come down here from heaven and manifest Himself as I worship Him. Through worship, I am tuning up myself to discover where I'm already living by the Spirit! This introduces a level of excitement and enthusiasm in worship that I would not otherwise know.

"But how," you might ask, "can I actually be joining heavenly worship in my finite locale? If God is truly omnipresent, how can His throne room really exist in my local church or my Bible study group?" That's one of the amazing things about God: He is so great that He is not even limited by His omnipresence. For God not only is everywhere at the same time but also can localize His manifestations in an infinite number of ways simultaneously! That is the greatness of our God. Our passion to worship God will be greatly enhanced when we understand that when we worship, we are quite literally joining the heavenly processional before the divine throne.

Dan Gardner

The Reverend Dan Gardner is minister of music at Zion Evangelistic Temple in Clawson, Michigan. He has been on the full-time pastoral staff since 1980 and has a bachelor's degree in music from Oakland University. Dan's worship songs, published through Integrity's  *Hosanna! Music, are well known internationally. Some of his most popular songs include "My Life Is in You, Lord," "Blessed Be the Rock," and "Exalt the Lord Our God." Dan was the featured worship leader on Integrity's Hosanna! Music's* Praise and Honor *recording. Some of Dan's choral works, including "We Have Overcome," are published through Tempo Music.*

Since 1981 Dan has ministered at worship/music conferences across the country, teaching on worship leading, songwriting, and other disciplines. His heart to see Christian musicians raised up to be a powerful influence both within and outside the church has led Dan to begin the Christian Musicians Network, the purpose of which is to train and equip musicians for ministry.

Dan, his wife, Joanne, and their two daughters live in Troy, Michigan.

SIMPLE PRAISE, SIMPLE SOLUTION

by Dan Gardner

~ Nearly every time I speak about the subject of worship, I tell about a personal encounter with the Lord that profoundly changed my personal worship and helped shape my underlying motivation for leading God's people in praise. This lesson came to me about twelve years ago through my daughter, Angela, when she was a vibrant three-year-old toddler.

Wednesday afternoons have been my prayer and preparation time for leading worship in our midweek service for over seventeen years. Typically, as on this day, I sat at the piano in my living room to prepare for the evening service. This particular afternoon I was struggling to come up with the all-important "worship list." I had prayed and spent time worshiping the Lord, reading the Word, and doing everything I would normally do to prepare—yet I was still coming up empty. Not a single song. As the clock kept moving forward, I began to sweat. 3:00. 4:00. 5:00. The clock kept ticking, but still nothing.

Becoming increasingly desperate, I started fumbling through my alphabetical song list to grab those songs that have worked in the past, or maybe, just maybe, the Lord would impress me with the right songs as I gazed at their titles.

I scanned through my 300-song list at least two or three times. Nothing! I looked through worship lists from past services. Nothing! I was dry. I have never enjoyed these dry spells (though they certainly teach one trust and reliance upon the Lord, don't they?). As far as I knew, there was no unconfessed sin to stand in the way. I was desperately trying to do my part by seeking God, truly wanting to get His heart for this worship service. This seemed much more overwhelming than it needed to be!

Frustrated and growing more anxious, I left the piano to go into the kitchen to get something to eat (my carnal reaction to stress). The kitchen in our home is adjacent to our family room. I was drawn away from the refrigerator and stepped toward the family room. As I walked to the edge of the room, an overwhelming sense of God's presence met me at the door.

As God's presence flooded my heart, I peered into the family room and noticed my three-year-old daughter Angela kneeling on our couch, looking out the picture window toward the heavens. Her eyes were fixed on something outside the window, and her hands were raised high. Angela was singing ever so quietly in her sweet little voice, "I love You, Jesus; I praise You, Jesus."

Tears flooded my eyes as I watched Angela pouring out her heart of love to the Master. In those moments, I enjoyed what I had been yearning for all afternoon. I had been just two rooms away!

I have never forgotten that experience. When I find myself striving and sweating to get into worship, this experience reminds me that the motivation for my personal worship and ministry is this: *I must allow the love that Christ deposited in my heart to flow back to Him in a nonpretentious, simple way.* As I rested in that love on that Wednesday night and many services since, I have found Him to be faithful to meet us.

David Garratt

David Garratt, along with his wife, Dale, pioneered Scripture in Song praise and worship music. For the past twenty-seven years David has been involved in recording and publishing praise and worship songs as well as teaching and leading many of God's people in worship throughout many parts of the world.

David is currently working with a number of indigenous groups, encouraging them to offer the treasures from their cultures to God.

David and Dale reside in New Zealand.

Drapes, Pews, and a Dancing Worship Leader

by David Garratt

~ **B**y 1982, after almost ten years of ministering in praise and worship and fourteen years after recording our first praise and worship tape, we were in some ways considered experts in a field that until then few others seemed to be a part of.

Dale and I had traveled to Europe, America, Asia, and Africa as well as around Australia and New Zealand, which are our home territories. We had led and taught in these places and felt we had some understanding of at least the basics.

Then, early in 1982, two men—one a Welshman and the other from Arkansas in the United States—visited New Zealand to do some teaching on prophecy and worship. We traveled as part of the ministering team, leading worship in various locations around the nation.

The problem for me was that the American was teaching on being free to "dance before the Lord"—not the sort of dance that's done by people skilled in creative movement but the sort that the newly crowned King David did before the Lord, leaping for joy in an unrestrained way.

This teaching shattered my status quo, to say the least! It challenged my spiritual equilibrium, breaking into my neatly constructed boxes of what was proper and what wasn't. Worst of all, I knew I heard God saying, "Unless you become like a little child you won't even enter . . . ."

At that time Dale and I were leading a group of worshipers at a local mainline church, and the things we were doing were considered radical enough without *this!* However, God helped us, and over the following months at our Tuesday-evening praise times at the local school auditorium, we found ourselves becoming free in spontaneous praise. These times even included expressions of dance. The crunch came one Sunday morning when we were leading worship from behind the large, polished, wooden podium. The auditorium was thickly carpeted, complete with heavy gold drapes and pews that were firmly bolted to the floor.

As always, the team had prepared the room by coming an hour early to pray and worship around the room, to invite the presence of the Holy Spirit in the service to follow. Unfortunately, even with this preparation, once the congregation was there we often struggled. I think the struggle was both with the religious spirit that loves to inhabit religious environments (especially on Sunday mornings) and with the acoustics in the room, which led me to firmly believe that the devil is an architect! Each musical note was literally swallowed by the carpet, drapes, and acoustic tiles on the ceiling.

That morning I began to lead a song of joyful praise, and many of the people joined in, clapping along with the rhythm. This wasn't unusual, but the next thing was. "Step out from behind the podium and dance," said a clear, unmistakable voice in my spirit.

"What?" I reasoned.

"Don't just sing about it. Do it," said the voice that I recognized as that of the Holy Spirit. I looked at the people, dressed in their Sunday best. "Dance before Me in front of them."

So, remembering the word about little children and feeling as foolish as a frog on a freeway, I stepped from behind the security of that podium and danced up and down across the front of the room. My joy was real and my heart sincere as I praised God with all my might.

Something broke in me that day. As I danced and others joined me, I realized that so often we talk and sing about what we are going to do in our praises, yet we need to "just do it." I also saw something of the truth of what the Levites said so many years before to a people weary with sin and deprivation: "The joy of the LORD is your strength" (Nehemiah 8:10).

Have you ever seen a child stand still while expressing true joy? Neither have I.

Chuck Girard

Chuck Girard is one of the pioneers of contemporary Christian music and continues to be a voice of the move of God in that field.

Born and raised in Southern California, Chuck began playing music at an early age, leading to a successful career as a studio singer and musician during the surf era of popular music.

Soon after this, Chuck began to realize his need for God. He began a five-year search for spiritual reality through psychedelic drugs, Eastern religions, and the like as he pursued a hippie lifestyle in the '60s. This search ended in a then-small church in Orange County, California, where Chuck found true spiritual reality through the gospel of Jesus Christ. After his new birth in 1970, he and four friends began ministry with the group Love Song. The group became the first group to play rock-oriented music in the Christian setting and to gain international acceptance and popularity in the early '70s revival known as the Jesus Movement.

After the disbanding of Love Song in 1974, Chuck continued to minister in a solo capacity, later that year releasing his first solo album, featuring his most popular song, "Sometimes Alleluia." Over the years Chuck has released many solo albums.

As well as continuing in his traveling ministry to the body of Christ, Chuck serves as an associate pastor and minister of music at Los Angeles Metrowest Christian Fellowship of West Los Angeles. Chuck currently resides in Chatsworth, California, with his wife, Karen, and their four daughters.

The Ways of the Spirit

by Chuck Girard

Back in the earliest days of my own discovery of worship, I had an experience that impacted me so profoundly that I have never been the same.

I had just come through a time of correction in my life and was seeking God with a new sense of urgency. God had given me two mandates that became the guideposts of this period of my life.

First, He had said to grow up! I'd been a child of God long enough; it was time to become a man of God. Second, He said that if I was going to continue to characterize myself as a Christian musician, I ought to see what *He* had to say about music. Hence an intense Bible study began that was to go on for some time, ultimately leading me into a discovery of worship from a biblical perspective.

Around this time, there was a particular instance when I was seeking God in prayer. Even though I sensed His presence, there seemed to be no connection with His purpose in this time of prayer. I had been a Christian long enough at this time to know that this was a good time to sit down and listen. As I did, before long I heard the still small voice of the Lord say to me, "Would you go to the piano and play a concert just for Me?"

Unbelievable as it sounds, I had never done this before. I had started out in secular music for ten years and had graduated immediately into the group Love Song as a Christian.

Music was my "gig," and it never occurred to me to just sit down and worship. Significantly, God had invited me to give just Him a concert. This was to turn into probably the most profound worship experience of my life.

I began with a songbook that was on my piano, not having ever sung an entire worship song through from memory. Then I turned the page and saw a lyric that expressed something that I felt in my heart, but I could not play it, because I did not know the melody. God prompted me to go ahead anyway, and He gave me a new melody for that lyric. Before long, I discarded the book and just began to sing freely to God, laughing and weeping almost at the same time.

This experience went on for some ninety minutes and was my first connection into the power of spontaneous worship. I didn't know the buzz words then, such as "song of the Lord," "psalmistry," "the secret place," "the inner court," but all these things were happening in this tender learning experience. Since then, God has continued to teach me the ways of the Spirit, and almost everything I learn to do in public comes out of my private times of worship as I seek God this way.

THE POWER OF SILENCE

by Chuck Girard

One of the things that I've always believed is that the maximum power of worship is not necessarily expressed in the more excitable type of celebration we often characterize as "good worship." This is not to say that we can't have a powerful experience that way, but as the Bible says in 1 Kings 19:11–13, the Lord wasn't in the wind, He wasn't in the fire, He wasn't in the earthquake. He was in the still small voice.

One time in the early days of what I was later to see as my personal revelation of worship, I had just finished a tape series on the value of edifying oneself by praying in the Spirit. On my way to a Sunday-morning service not too far from where I live, I decided to give this principle a trial run by praying in the Spirit all the way to the meeting, which was about a one-and-a-half-hour drive. About ten minutes from my destination, I stopped and asked the Lord for a word for the church that morning.

Immediately I heard the voice of the Lord say to me, "When you get on the platform this morning, be absolutely silent for fifteen minutes. I will do the rest." This was not an easy word to receive, as you can imagine. I was invited in as guest speaker/musician, and my reputation at that time was primarily for my musical gift. Silence was not what most people were expecting that morning.

I immediately started what I jokingly call the "Abrahamic negotiations"—"Lord, would you bless for ten minutes of silence? Lord, what about even five minutes? That's still a long time." Then I went into some doctrinal tweaking: "Well, five minutes is a long time of silence. Perhaps God didn't mean a literal fifteen minutes. Perhaps five will get the job done."

My sense of discomfort ruled over my sense of obedience for a time, and I had pretty well decided that I could get away with a meditative four or five minutes of silence and then sing some slow tunes to get into worship. But it was not to be. The second I set foot on the platform, as clearly as I've ever heard anything from the Lord, He said, "Well, you do what you want, but you know what I said!"

Dutifully, I faced the people and shared with them what I believed the Lord to be instructing. Quickly I took a seat on the piano bench facing the wall, head in hands, assuming a holy-looking position as I began to die a thousand deaths.

I'll never get invited back here, I thought, as well as the very spiritual, *There won't be much of an offering today!*

During the first five minutes, I could almost hear people thinking out loud, "What is this guy doing? I didn't come to church to be silent; I came to hear the Word," or any variation of an infinite amount of like comments. But *after* the first five minutes, a hush settled on the place as the presence of God began to fill the room. You could sense the deep work of God as He pried into the parched hearts of many who probably hadn't taken five minutes to listen to God or bask in His presence in quite some time.

After the second five minutes, God began to impress me to walk into the crowd and deliver some words of knowledge: "God wants you to know that He has seen your pain, and He's not forsaken you. You've kept your heart right, and God is about to bring deliverance." People began to weep as God touched their hearts with His comfort and love.

After I got back to the piano, I started to sing a couple of slow songs, working my way to some worship choruses as the people began to join in. The music built and crescendoed, and by the end of the service we were singing the victory songs and "rocking out"!

This was one of my most challenging experiences in trying to obey the voice of the Lord unconditionally. It is also my most profound experience even to the present time in seeing the power of silence in action.

Gerrit Gustafson

Gerrit Gustafson is a Bible teacher, songwriter, and advocate of whole-hearted worship. Gerrit conducts seminars and conferences throughout the nation and abroad through Kingdom of Priests Ministries.

Having served Integrity's Hosanna! Music as music coordinator, creative team consultant, and songwriter, Gerrit has written over forty songs that have been recorded by Integrity. These songs include "There's Glory All Around," "Unto You," "Have Mercy on Me," "Only by Grace," "Into Your Courts," and "I Hear Angels." He is also involved in developing resources for worship in small groups.

Apprehended by God's call during his college years, Gerrit served as pastor and teacher for fifteen years in churches in Colorado, Florida, Mississippi, and Alabama. Gerrit and his wife, Himmie, have five children and live in Mobile, Alabama.

THE FIRST TIME

by Gerrit Gustafson

I remember the first time that music deeply affected me. It was in Ft. Payne, Alabama, in the late '50s. I was about ten. My older sister Gwen brought home a record of the song "Theme from a Summer Place" with the Percy Faith Orchestra. The first time I heard it was like meeting someone you really want to get to know. Then and there, I made my plans to listen to it all by myself sometime when Gwen was gone.

The time came. We weren't into sharing back them, so I had to do some sneaking around to locate the hidden treasure. When I found it, I convinced myself that Gwen wouldn't mind my broadening my cultural boundaries. I reverently took the 45 (no, that's not a handgun; it's a kind of record they used to have) out to our living room to play on our old Magnavox.

Remember how you had to put the attachment on the spindle to play those 45s? And how you could move the arm off the record and the song would repeat over and over? Well, when I had it all set, I turned it on, lay on the floor with my feet propped up on the wall, and drank in every note.

I'm sure you remember how the combination of those slow eighth-note triplets, the sweet strings sounds, the horns, and that haunting melody line would just get under you and carry you off to some distant place. It had the same effect on me, too. It was my first high. I was mesmerized. I didn't want it to stop. But when it did, it would just start over again. And again and again. The only thing I had to worry about was the return of the big sister.

That first time of tasting the power of music was the beginning of a long relationship. School bands, stage bands, Dixieland jazz, popular jazz, and then studying composition at Florida State University. That first taste at age ten was the first step of a journey to make music my life.

And then there was the first time I encountered the power of worship. It was in Tallahassee, Florida, in the late '60s. I was about twenty. About a year before, I had become a Christian through the faithful persistence of my college roommate Bob Sutton. We used to have Bible studies in dorms or apartments, so it wasn't unusual that we were going to hear a Bible teacher in the meeting room of a bank building.

There were about two hundred people there that night. Everyone seemed so enthusiastic and so genuinely glad to see one another. Derek Prince was the guest speaker.

Derek's English accent punctuated everything he said with such clarity and authority. Looking around at everybody's rapt attention, I was impressed that what we were doing was probably very similar to the activities of the early New Testament church.

But what was about to take place transcended our time and space orientation even more. When the message was over, someone stood up and said something like, "Let's just lift our voices in praise." Maybe we sang some songs—I don't remember—but I do remember something happening that absolutely penetrated the core of my being.

At some point in the singing, those two hundred people began to sound like an ethereal symphony of voices warming up. I remember analyzing the sound: it was very polyphonic—many different melody lines going on simultaneously; it was arrhythmic—almost no rhythmic definition; and there was no chord progression—all of the singing held together around a major chord with added 6ths and 2nds.

I remember how the sounds would swell to a great and jubilant tone, and then, almost as if there were an invisible conductor, the sounds would subside, leaving us in a state of expectancy as though God were about to whisper something to our hearts. At one such point, two female voices rose above the heavenly hum and created the most lovely little duet I think I have ever heard.

Talk about being carried away! I didn't have a category for this music. Maybe I had missed something in my music history class! And when did all these people get together to rehearse for this? Do they have this music at the record store? The only word I could find to describe it was "heavenly." I decided, "This must be what worship sounds like in heaven."

I'm not ashamed to say that I'm hooked. Twenty-five years later, I'm still addicted. I have tasted the powers of the age to come (Hebrews 6:5). And that first time was not the last time. I have heard that heavenly sound again and again. That first encounter led me to a decision: More than anything, I wanted to be around that sound and that atmosphere for the rest of my life. I want my music and my whole life to adapt to that sound. I want it to be on earth as it is in heaven!

Somewhere I read a true story of a man who had devoted himself to the study of insects. He was what is known as an entomologist. Once, when he was several weeks into the study of a certain insect in one of the western states, the shadow of a great bird caused him to look up and see an eagle. He was captivated as he watched this eagle navigate effortlessly on the wind. He estimated that it was a full eight minutes and several miles of flight before he saw that eagle flap its wings the first time. "This," he observed, "is an amazing animal!"

After that experience, the entomologist lost his interest in insects. From that point on, he devoted the rest of his life to the study of eagles!

Likewise, the first time music really spoke to me through my sister's 45 on our family's Magnavox was the first step in a journey to make music my life. But the first time I encountered the heavenly sounds of worship was the introduction to something even more wondrous—living life as a worshiper in the presence of God. And for that discovery, I am eternally grateful!

Dennis Jernigan

Dennis Jernigan is a worship leader who believes his calling in life is to lead others to a heart-to-heart confrontation with the Lord Jesus Christ through his music. He has written hundreds of songs, including "You  *Are My All in All," "Nobody Fills My Heart Like Jesus," "Thank You," and "We Will Worship the Lamb of Glory," which are sung literally all over the world.*

Born and raised on a small Oklahoma farm near the town of Boynton, Dennis was reared in the Southern Baptist faith. He discovered at an early age that he had a very special gift from the Lord—he could hear music and then reproduce what he heard on the piano. By the time he was nine years old, he was regularly playing the piano during the service at First Baptist Church in Boynton.

Dennis seeks to bring the message of hope and healing to the body of Christ through the worship of the almighty God. He believes worship is all about relationship rather than performance, and he desires to help people get honest with themselves and with God because he has found in his own life that honesty and truth have set him free.

Dennis and his wife, Melinda, are the proud parents of nine (!) children. They make their home in Muskogee, Oklahoma, where they serve Christ through the local body of believers known as New Community Church.

THE MAKING OF A WORSHIP LEADER
by Dennis Jernigan

~&& **A**s I look back over my life and admit where I have failed, it becomes easier to see how knowledge of the truth has set me free. Who I am, my identity as a worshiper and as a worship leader, has been shaped by the truths as well as the lies I have believed.

I was raised in the Southern Baptist denomination. From the time I was nine years old, I was the church pianist. Because I felt I had to perform for my father's acceptance and approval, I also felt that this was the way I must respond to God: to "do right" so He would love me.

Another contributing factor in my journey toward finding my identity was the fact that I struggled with my sexual identity—with homosexuality—from my earliest memories. Because I saw how the church responded to this particular sin (not in love), my heart was bound in a prison of fears and lies. This only helped feed my need to perform. I had to be the best at everything so everyone would like me. I started on the basketball team in each year of high school. I was valedictorian of my senior class (of thirteen!). I led out in school and church activities and anything else that could bolster my self-esteem. Going away to college left me alone and open to an ever-deepening cycle of sin and performance that never seemed to satisfy, and I began to wonder whether intimacy with God was really possible.

After graduating from a well-known Southern Baptist university with not a clue as to my purpose in life, I had come to the bottom of my heart's well concerning my personal struggle with homosexuality and my identity. I was basically ready to give up on life and, subsequently, on God. Fortunately, God saw fit to give me some time off for the purpose of dealing with these issues. You may be wondering, "What in the world does this have to do with leading worship?" That is a valid question. But in my estimation, this was the beginning of a ministry for which I had no personal aspirations, one of which I had no concept—the ministry of leading others into intimacy with the Father.

If you have worked toward a music degree or know someone who has, you will understand this glimpse of God's sense of humor. God moved me to live with a family in Oklahoma City. The only job I could get was that of a school bus driver! While this seemed desperate to me at first, I soon came to realize God's wisdom. I had an early-morning route and an afternoon route, with several hours to kill in between. Because I had no clues as to my identity and because I had no one else to teach me, I simply put my Bible on my piano during those in-between hours, turned to the book of Psalms, and did what David did. I simply got honest with God.

In the mornings I actually had two bus routes, with twenty-five minutes between those routes. During those twenty-five minutes, I would park my bus in an abandoned housing addition and write in my journal. This journal was the method I found most helpful in getting my deepest, darkest, and most intimate thoughts—about anything—out in the open to God. Day in and day out I wrote of hurts, disillusionments, failures, emotions, and any other soul data I found needing to come out. What I discovered in the process was that God really was concerned with my feelings, whatever they might be and however dark they might seem to me. I found God approachable and desirous of my presence. In fact, I began to understand that God took more delight in my presence than I could possibly take in His! After that first year of keeping a journal, I felt God impress me to burn it. Page by page I burned my deepest heart cries and most horrendous secrets. Gently and tenderly, Father God taught me that just as this picture of my past was being burned away, so too, He had cleansed me of my past—and present and future—and forever forgave and forgot the wickedness of my heart.

I continued to cry out to Him from the piano day by day, many times literally in tears, because I had tried to live for God so many times in the past, only to fall deeper and deeper into the trenches of sin. My concept of God was that of a cosmic policeman—a distant God waiting for me to mess up so that He could step back into my life and bop me on the head. I felt ashamed and unworthy of His love. I felt that God was unapproachable. Still, I could not yet give up.

Day by day, as I cried out to God, I began doing what I saw David had done. Not only did I become bluntly honest with my God, but also I began to write down my prayers, which, for me, happened to come out in the form of songs! Soon I came to realize that God's love for me was based not on how well I performed in this life but upon my recognition of His abiding presence in my life, no matter how deeply in sin I had fallen and no matter how inconsistent I was in my love for Him. My heart was broken when I realized that there was nothing I could do to earn His love, because He loved me no matter what!

This truth was brought to the forefront of my heart through the ministry of The Second Chapter of Acts. During one of their concerts, Annie Herring shared that God had shown her that there was someone present who carried something so shameful in his or her heart that that person would be devastated if he or she thought anyone knew about it. She shared that God knew—and that He loved that person anyway. I knew that someone was me. By faith I lifted my sin to Jesus and told Him that I could not overcome it but that I would let Him carry it away for me. As Second Chapter sang

"Mansion Builder," I saw my sin placed upon Christ, myself crucified and buried with Him and my sin. And I saw Him risen and calling me to come forth and be someone brand-new! That night, the power of that sin was broken in my life, and the worship and songs began to pour out like a river!

As the songs began to flow, I began to look for others to sing them to and to sing them with. I soon realized that if I simply entered boldly into God's presence, it did not matter whether others followed me. Two things quickly became apparent to me. First, I realized that my job was simply to seek God's heart. Second, I understood that the Good Shepherd never beat His sheep or forced them to worship Him. As I became more and more free in my expression to Him, others seemed to be drawn to Him *with* me.

Around this time, another godly family had taken me under their wings. They began to encourage me to worship God in ways this Southern Baptist boy had only heard about. What I found was that God had given me a body to use in expressing my heart. He gave me emotions with which to express my feelings. And above all else, He showed me that He was worthy of all my love, because He had literally borne all my sins on the cross.

As I began writing down my prayers, it became a very natural progression to share those songs with my friends. It was quite overwhelming when they seemed to take the songs and sing them as their own. It was during many nights around the piano that I first learned to express my heart in openness and honesty to the Lord in a corporate setting. It was also here that I began to realize that a person's response to God was not my responsibility. It is each person's choice. I realized that I need not try to coerce anyone to praise God.

A few short years later, I found myself working as a church janitor/secretary. One Sunday the music minister said that God had shown him that he was standing in the wrong place and that Dennis Jernigan was to be leading the worship. That very day I led worship for the first time for a large group of people and found my calling in life—to help others know Jesus Christ in an intimate and deep way through worship.

Just as God so faithfully met with me in my first feeble and awkward attempts at communing with Him, He has been faithful to lead me deeper and deeper into an ever-growing, vibrant, living relationship with a living God. The one thing I would say to anyone concerning leading worship is this: seek God for yourself. Seek Him and not a ministry. Find Him, and ministry will come as a natural overflow of the life lived seeking Him. He will be as near as we need Him to be.

In leading others to worship Him I simply seek Him myself and encourage those who desire to meet with Him to go with me. I don't worry whether they follow or not. The way I see it, just as God was so faithful to meet me where I was, He can do the same for anyone else who genuinely recognizes his or her need and then sets out to seek Him in whatever way he or she knows.

Why do I worship? I cannot help myself. I see where I would be had it not been for Jesus Christ. Worship begins in the heart. Anything outward is simply an extension of what's on the inside. At best, we see through a glass dimly. And, yes, one day we will see Him face to face.

The following helps to explain my definition of a worshiper and of a worship leader:

Here is my heart, Lord. Wipe off as much of the grime and dust that separates me from You as You can in this life so there is no big change when I finally step into eternity. A life lived with the heart exposed to the Light is the life of a worshiper. And this truly is a worship leader—one who shares that heart and lives out that heart before others.

Bob Kauflin

After receiving a piano performance degree from Temple University in 1976, Bob Kauflin traveled for eight years with the contemporary Christian group Glad as a writer, speaker, and arranger. In 1984 he left the group to pursue involvement in the local church. Although he continues to write for Glad, his growing passion since that time has been worship.

Bob is Director of Worship Development for Sovereign Grace Ministries, a family of 60-plus churches led by C.J. Mahaney. His responsibilities include equipping pastors and musicians in the theology and practice of con-gregational worship and contributing to Sov-ereign Grace recordings, including Upward: The Bob Kauflin Hymns Project *and, most recently,* Worship God Live.

Bob also serves as the music and worship pastor for Covenant Life Church in Gaithersburg, Maryland, led by Josh Harris. Many of Bob's teachings can be found at www.sovgracemin.org. Bob also writes a five-day-a-week blog at www.worshipmatters.com.

He loves his wife of 29 years, Julie, passionately. Bob and Julie have six children and four grandchildren.

HAPPY BIRTHDAY TO YOU

by Bob Kauflin

The song of the Lord, or prophetic singing, is an area of worship that has intrigued me ever since I learned of its existence about ten years ago. By "song of the Lord," I'm referring especially to spontaneous songs that reflect God's heart toward His people or spontaneous songs that are sung corporately to God.

One of the more memorable songs the Lord gave me came during a worship-group rehearsal years ago. We had been focusing on the sovereign rule of Jesus, and I was overwhelmed with the thought of Jesus having the name above all names and being so worthy of our worship. In the midst of our worship, I began singing, "You have been given the name above all names, and we worship You, yes we worship You." Gradually the group picked it up, and we had a wonderful time worshiping together with a spontaneous song. After that, I was open to singing spontaneously during worship as I felt led. However, I failed to step out consistently because of doubts about my motives. "Why do I want to do this? Do I want to make a good impression on everyone? What if I go blank in the middle of a phrase? What if my song has no effect on anyone?" Accusations and discouraging thoughts generally kept me quiet, except for the rare occasion when I had a very strong impression.

In 1992, while at a leaders' conference, God graciously broke through my dull heart with the truth that my duty was simply to obey His voice, not to predict the effect of my prophetic song or to second-guess my motives. God showed me that my heart would never be *entirely* pure, so I could be released to obey His voice while trusting Him to expose and change any wrong motives. I experienced a release of prophetic songs almost immediately. What a relief to know that God Himself was responsible for not only the impression but also the fruit.

Later that year, this lesson was driven home at another conference in Indiana, Pennsylvania. About three thousand men, women, and children had gathered from different churches related through People of Destiny International, led by C.J. Mahaney, for a weekend of worship, ministry, and teaching. During one of the last worship sessions, C.J. came up to the microphone to apologetically explain how he had been struggling all weekend with a word he felt the Lord had wanted him to speak. He acknowledged that he had to give it, no matter how foolish it might seem. "I'd like everyone whose birthday is in May to please stand up. I believe the Lord wants to minister to you." In the next moments, I distinctly felt that the Lord was giving me a song for those who were standing. Everything seemed fine and under control until I thought God was telling me that the climax of the song was going to be the words, "So Happy Birthday to you. Happy Birthday, My chosen ones. I have loved you for all time." I remember thinking, "If I go through with this, either the heavens are going to open or my friends will never let me live this down." With fear and trepidation, I forged ahead. Regardless of the consequences, I knew I had to obey what I thought to be the voice of the Lord.

Reports came back in the following weeks of how God had ministered to various people through that prophetic song. One woman had been adopted as a child and had never been able to forgive her parents for abandoning her. For the first time God broke through her unforgiveness in a tangible way, and she felt His love wash away her sense of rejection and feeling forsaken. A pastor related that it was one of the most significant times of ministry he had experienced.

Many of those at the session had stood weeping as God's love was freshly shed abroad in their hearts. Had these people been affected through some brilliant, finely crafted spontaneous song, I might have tried to take some credit. But what touched their hearts and broke down their defenses was someone singing "Happy Birthday." I learned then, as I continue to learn, that God is not impressed with my gifts or abilities. He gave them to me. What He is interested in is my humility leading to obedience. My protests notwithstanding, if God can use Balaam's donkey, He can use me to speak to others. The matter is not how profound or unique my words are but how faithful I am to speak or sing them when God gives them to me.

Monty Kelso

Monty Kelso has been Director of Creative Communication and worship leader at Coast Hills Community Church in Aliso Viejo, California, since its beginning in the mid-1980s. As well as leading a dynamic creative team at Coast Hills (a Willow Creek Association church), he is a worship leader for Maranatha! Music and continues to lead one of Maranatha's Worship Leader Workshop teams. He regularly participates in various conferences throughout the U.S. as a worship leader and conference speaker.

A passion for effective teams that creatively communicate Jesus Christ through the arts is evident whether you attend the Coast Hills Creative Communications conference, attend one of Monty's workshops, talk to Monty on the phone, or read his articles found in Worship Leader magazine.

Monty sums up his life by saying, "It's all about relationships—finding ways to help others (and myself) continue to grow and enjoy relationship with God, family, the church family, and people in general."

Monty, his wife, Christa, and their three sons, Conner, Trevor, and Bryson, live in Laguna Beach, California.

GETTING A GRIP ON LETTING GO
by Monty Kelso

~≈**W**hen my wife and I helped launch a new church plant called Coast Hills Community Church in the mid-1980s, I was young, without children, mildly experienced, and ready to tackle just about anything of a pioneering nature. Especially when "the call" required that we move to the beach and settle in San Clemente, California (whose license plate frames read "World's Best Climate"). The idea of starting a new church unencumbered by the web of former staff and tradition was a long-time dream—finally a place where my passion for creative worship could be realized. Add to this ideal situation the fact that the senior pastor and his wife, Denny and Leesa Bellesi, shared this same dream. In fact, Leesa was a seasoned dancer and choreographer, and Denny was a product of Youth For Christ and two of the most creative churches in Southern California. Needless to say we had vision far beyond our initial capacity. Here we were, a start-from-scratch, interdenominational community church with little financial support and only a handful of enthusiastic people. What we did have going for us were the right people at the right time in the right place and a mighty God who desired to build His church in the growing community of south Orange County, California.

Like many other church plants, our "portable church" set up camp at a local high school. Every Sunday morning at daybreak a team of able-bodied volunteers would transform Dana Hills High School in Dana Point into a sanctuary of worship.

Volunteers set up classrooms for the children, sound and lighting systems, staging, signs, refreshments, and three hundred feet of curtains that tied onto the second-story railing encompassing our meeting hall. Volunteers showed up every Sunday to play, sing, act, hang visuals, usher, greet, serve donuts, and host the information center. It was my job to see that all this happened without a hitch each week.

From the beginning we placed a high value on communicating with excellence and authenticity, and that value spread to every fiber of the church. We worked hard to ensure that this value was reflected everywhere one looked. I was personally driven to give God our best no matter the cost. This drive reflected not only in the product of worship but also in the process. My week was soon filled up with countless meetings, leading volunteers down this new path of contemporary worship. I then thought I knew exactly how things should be done. After all, I saw the big picture and was the only one who could possibly know the right way to make things happen. The grip I held on my ministry was strengthening as I saw empty chairs filling up over the rapidly passing months. I figured we must have been doing this right, because people kept coming.

It wasn't that I did everything myself. I had put together a creative planning team within the first year of ministry. I had identified point leaders for each of the teams. I even left for six weeks within the first year to do an overseas ministry project. It seemed that all was going well, the way God had intended. After all, He was blessing my hard work with a growing church and growing ministry team. There was no denying that Coast Hills had my signature all over it. My dreams were being realized.

Fast-forward seven years. It was the early nineties. My wife and I had managed to find time to start our family. The church had grown significantly to three services, and we were rapidly outgrowing the high school. I had squeezed out of the general budget enough money to hire a part-time music director and a part-time assistant but was still holding a tight grip on the details of what was then called the Celebration Arts ministry. The time had come for Coast Hills to find its own permanent location, and quickly the pursuit began. Meanwhile, the demands of programming and rehearsing every week's service were ever before us. By now a host of other special events and projects had been added to the annual diet of this entrepreneur-led church. It's accurate to say that at this point most of us were, by our own initiative, overworked and underpaid and loving every minute of it. The lack of material resources was compensated by a wealth of human resources with talent that surpassed anyone's wildest expectations. This may have been the very factor that set me up for the big shutdown to come.

In 1993, after two years of praying, planning, praying, conducting capital campaigns, designing buildings, and praying some more, we, by God's grace, squeaked into our new 1500-seat auditorium in Aliso Viejo. The building was designed as a community theater in an effort to build a bridge between the arts community and the church. What we hadn't planned on was that the major budget cutbacks at the eleventh hour of construction would impact mostly the auditorium audiovisuals. With the exception of some expensive wiring and a bare-bones lighting system, we were reduced to a road-weary sound system and an unlimited supply of duct tape. Yet the expectation fostered by this magnificent new building left both the congregation and the community waiting for the *next level* of dynamic communication. No pressure!

After years of hoping and dreaming for our own building and all the solutions it would bring to our never-ending complexities of being a portable church, it suddenly became the very catalyst that would lead me to the end of myself.

It was a combination of several factors, which are continually becoming clearer to me, that nearly drove my team and me over the edge. I realize now that nearly all of them are rooted in the sin of pride. A relentless pursuit of excellence that was not only a positive reflection of God's church but also a positive reflection on me kept me driving forward, no matter how steep the climb. My identity and source of gratification became the successes of the Celebration Arts ministry. In some ways my ministry became my god. I worshiped the successes along the way. I found great satisfaction in a plan that worked. I had confused who the object of my worship was.

The defining moment was on an ordinary weekend when I realized that my ability to worship God was totally conditional. My personal satisfaction level with the service determined it. How profound was the flow of the service? What was the performance quality of the artists? Was the technician's execution of the plan flawless? Anything less than perfection left me frustrated, depressed, and unable to worship God authentically.

Not only was God offended with these offerings of "filthy rags," but also it had become clear to my team that I cared much more about the product than I cared about them. My grip on the ministry was so tight that even though I delegated responsibility, I didn't trust. Even though I included others, I didn't value their input. Even though I ran things by others, I still did what I wanted to do. What's ironic is that, for the most part, what I "went to the mat" over was all worthwhile and, under healthy circumstances, the right thing. After all, we were pioneering a new model church that received its fair share of criticism. It was easy to justify my actions for the sake of the cause. I had a way of making anyone who disagreed with me second-guess his or her conviction and leave the conversation confused and frustrated. This only fostered hostility in those few with whom I worked most closely.

In an effort to cope with the extreme stress of this season of our still growing church and a leader who was on a road to destruction, people began to talk amongst themselves and compare notes. As you can imagine, perceptions were embellished and my shortcomings were intensified. This was not a happy camp!

To the credit of my long-time pastor and partner in ministry, a meeting was called. Denny had invited anyone and everyone involved in leadership within the realm of my ministry to his house to get to the root of all the layers of stuff that had been accumulating over the previous months.

I'll never forget that August evening in 1993 when about fifteen people gathered to lovingly confront me as they saw me on the verge of spinning out and becoming another ministry casualty. It was in that painful process of hearing the perceptions and feelings of those whom I had gone to battle with that I began to realize my controlling behavior. It was in those few focused minutes that God convicted me of my sin. It was in that moment of brokenness that God showed me that I cared far too much about the organization of the church and its mission, vision, and values. I cared far too little about the things that mattered most: to love God with all my heart, soul, mind, and strength and to love others more than myself. It was at that moment that I committed to loosen the grip I had had on my ministry and to learn to serve those whom I lead, even when it means letting people or programs fail.

Today when I worship God, I have a profound appreciation of His grace. Whether I worship Him privately or publicly, I am reminded that He is most pleased when I offer Him my best, derived from a pure heart—a heart that is holy and blameless before Him, a heart that holds things loosely because I know that God is in charge. I now know that more than any model, program, plan, or production . . . people matter the most!

Graham Kendrick

Graham Kendrick's songs and hymns are sung by millions of people in numerous languages around the world. Some of his best-known songs include "Shine, Jesus, Shine," "Rejoice, Rejoice, Christ Is in You," and "Amazing Love." He is a cofounder of March for Jesus, which went global in 1994 with about ten million people participating.

A self-taught guitarist, Graham began writing and performing his songs during his teenage years and, after training as a teacher, ventured out full-time in music at the age of twenty-two.

He and his wife, Jill, have four daughters and live in South London.

LORD, I'M EMPTY

by Graham Kendrick

In Psalm 103 the psalmist applies his will to stir his whole being. "Praise the Lord, O my soul; all my inmost being, praise his holy name. Praise the Lord, O my soul, and forget not all his benefits." He is talking to himself, stirring himself into action. He is, as it were, shaking himself by his own lapels, picking himself up out of his own slumber and/or apathy, and demanding obedience of all his faculties. The discipline of worship requires that we stand in complete readiness for obedience to the Spirit, like a soldier preparing himself for action.

I clearly recall an occasion when this lesson was firmly printed on my mind. I had been invited to lead worship at a church some hours' drive away from home, so my wife and I set off early that morning in the rather ramshackle Morris 1000 van we had at the time. The weather was cold and icy, and the wind blew freely through the many gaps and holes in the vehicle!

I was in a grumpy mood and proceeded reluctantly, creating tension between my wife and me. At the time, I was spiritually dry and had no desire or motivation to travel such a long way, let alone to lead worship! By the time we arrived, my mood was blacker, the tension tauter, and the temperature colder.

For the duration of the last five minutes prior to facing the crowd of enthusiastic would-be praisers, I knew I faced a stark choice: Would I get right with the Lord and my wife (and the car!) and go on in raw faith, or would I be honest with my hosts and back out?

Probably motivated at least in part by pride, I decided on the former course of action. I confessed my sin, apologized to my wife, and stepped into the meeting, saying to the Lord something to the effect of, "Lord, I'm empty. I don't feel like worshiping You. I have nothing to give to You or with which to lead the people unless You give it to me. But, sink or swim, here I go!"

From the moment I began to lead the praise, my heart filled up and we praised with freedom and joy. I did not have to pretend or put on an act. Because I had determined to praise, the Lord ignited praise within me, and I genuinely overflowed.

At times I would like to forget that lesson. Usually those times are when I am not leading but instead am part of the congregation and feeling similarly fed up and grumpy. I would like to use my mood as a legitimate excuse not to join in, but (to the irritation of the less noble side of me) I now know that my feelings need not rule my spirit.

Adapted from Graham Kendrick, *Learning to Worship as a Way of Life* (Minneapolis, Minn.: Bethany House Publishers, 1984). Used by permission.

Bob Kilpatrick

Few contemporary Christian praise songs make it to the "classic" category. At least two of Bob Kilpatrick's songs are there—"Lord, Be Glorified" and "Here Am I (Send Me to the Nations)." Though these  *songs keep popping up on the greatest hits lists, there are many other tunes for which Bob is known: "Won by One," "Sold Out and Radical," and "I Will Not Be Ashamed" among them. His song "Bring Them Home" was sung at Mother Teresa's funeral service in Calcutta, India.*

Bob has been in full-time music and ministry since 1970. Over the years he has co-labored with a veritable Christian who's who, including Dr. Jack Hayford, Dr. Lloyd John Ogilvie, Corrie ten Boom, Michael W. Smith, dcTalk, Anne Graham Lotz, Keith Green, and Andraé Crouch. He produces recordings, working with artists like Phil Keaggy, Randy Stonehill, Sara Groves, and Noel Paul Stookey (of Peter, Paul & Mary). He has performed and spoken at many national conferences and music festivals.

The nationwide KLove radio network airs Bob's "Time Out with Bob Kilpatrick" devotional program three times daily. Bob writes a column for Christian Musician *magazine. His writings also have appeared on worshiptogether.com, on crosswalk.com, and in* Youth Specialties, CCM, *and* Relevant *magazines.*

In his latest project, This Changes Everything, *a multimedia concert experience, Bob has pulled the covers off his own life and delivered a very personal account of his own spiritual odyssey.*

He is married to Cindy, his high-school girlfriend. Together they have five children and live in Fair Oaks, California.

Cloud of Witnesses

by Bob Kilpatrick

❧ **M**y dad spent his early years in the stately but austere Orphan House in Charleston, South Carolina. In his teens he worked at the naval shipyard there and, like the prodigal son, spent his life in "riotous living." But after my dad's World War II stint in the Army Air Corps as a flight engineer, God got ahold of my dad. He felt a call to the ministry and spent the rest of his life touching those who, like him, had no place to call home but the house of God.

I remember falling asleep in the front pew as my dad preached in the churches he'd planted in rural Georgia. I remember potlucks after church under the shade of pine trees, eating fried chicken, black-eyed peas, and watermelon and drinking sweet tea. Later we traveled the world as my dad served as a chaplain in the Air Force. In his retirement years he and my mom made many missionary trips around the world and touched the lives of thousands of people.

My dad died unexpectedly on July 13, 1991. Of course, we all miss him. But we believe in the resurrection and in heaven. My dad has joined the "cloud of witnesses" written about in Hebrews.

I like that biblical metaphor because I have a frequently recurring image that crosses my mind when I am in concert. Sometimes I will back away from the microphone after a song, and while the audience applauds, I'll "see" my dad in the cloud of witnesses, cheering me on. It gives me a great deal of encouragement to think that he has preceded me and is applauding my efforts.

But the question I ask myself is this: What have I done that is worthy of applause in heaven? Maybe the cloud of witnesses like my songs. Maybe they laugh at my anecdotes. Maybe they are moved by my stories. I don't know, maybe all of the above. And maybe none of the above.

Perhaps what moves the cloud of witnesses are things I overlook or can't see—the kind word spoken to the exasperated flight attendant, the simple and sincere prayer offered before the concert by a young volunteer, the sudden burst of spiritual illumination that comes to someone as he or she finally realizes and experiences the depth of the love God has for him or her, the hug a child gives me after the concert is over and everyone is going home.

What gets a rousing response in heaven? What makes the cloud of witnesses rise up with a shout of joy? We who trust in Jesus and lay our hope in the resurrection also believe this: that there is a great difference between the value systems of heaven and those of earth. Sometimes we count our successes in numbers of people at our concerts or numbers of units sold of our recordings or dollars earned or articles written or awards received or applause given. However, maybe a more vital question is this: Are the cloud of witnesses cheering us on in these things, or are they waiting for something else? Perhaps lots of something else—the character of Christ growing in us, the pursuit of holiness, the giving of care to "the least of these," the sacrifice of praise, the commitment to God and God alone. You can add to this list yourself.

Jesus said that we would be judged by every idle word we speak. Did He speak that as a threat or as a reminder to us to see each word as possibly an eternally damning indictment? Or could He have meant simply that our character slips out in the unguarded moments and the unplanned actions, in the words that we don't premeditate? Could it be that what we do "for show"—and what is often loudly cheered by earthly onlookers—is dismissed in heaven in favor of the smaller, private expressions of His love. Tell me, what part of my life gets the best response from my dad and the rest of the cloud of witnesses—and from Jesus?

I visited Mother Teresa's Home for the Destitute and Dying in Calcutta, India, on two occasions. Each time I was impressed with the tender love the staff showed to the dying beggars who lay gaunt and passive on the rows of beds. I sat on the edge of a bed and sang to forty abandoned boys in the Calcutta Mission of Mercy Boys' Home. I thought about my dad at their age in the Charleston Orphan House. I could see him in the cloud of witnesses. And while those boys and I laughed and sang, I think I heard my dad cheering me on.

Tom Kraeuter

Tom Kraeuter (pronounced Kroyter) is one of the most prolific authors and teachers in the contemporary worship scene today. People of all ages receive new insights from his straightforward, humorous style.

Tom regularly ministers in Bible-believing churches of all types. From Assemblies of God to Presbyterian, Baptist to Pentecostal, Vineyard to Mennonite, the response is always overwhelmingly positive.

As an author, Tom has a dozen books to his credit, including Keys to Becoming an Effective Worship Leader *and* Guiding Your Church Through a Worship Transition, *available in bookstores worldwide. He is the former managing editor of* Psalmist *magazine, and his writings have appeared in nationally recognized periodicals.*

Some of Tom's favorite downtime activities include reading to his children, cooking, playing table tennis, and eating chocolate.

Since 1978 Tom has been a part of Christian Outreach Church near St. Louis, Missouri. He and his wife, Barbara, and their three children, David, Stephen, and Amy, reside in Hillsboro, Missouri.

THE DEADLY DISEASE OF PERFECTIONISM

by Tom Kraeuter

"What's the matter with you?" my wife asked.

"Nothing."

"Excuse me, but I know you better than that. Now, what's wrong?"

"Okay, okay," I responded. "Everything went wrong in the service this morning."

"*Everything* went wrong? I can't remember *anything* being wrong."

"Where were you? The transition between 'Holy, Holy, Holy' and 'Blessed Be the Lord God Almighty' was awful. The drummer missed the endings of two songs. And our monitors were not working at all when we went back up after the sermon. The whole service was a catastrophe!"

My wife smiled. "Let me get this straight," she replied. "All but one transition went well, the drummer did great except for the ending of two songs, and the monitors worked well except for the closing song. Is that correct?"

"Well, yeah, I guess."

"So really almost everything went *right*." Her smile broadened. "Right?"

"Oh, you just don't understand."

In retrospect I have realized that it was I who didn't understand. It took me a long time to admit it, but I suffer from a potentially deadly affliction that plagues many worship leaders: perfectionism. Statistics indicate that nearly five out of every five worship leaders have it. If you have this horrendous dis-ease, you know exactly what I'm talking about. It can sap your strength and steal your joy. If ninety-nine things go right and one goes wrong, the only thing you remember is the one that went wrong.

Services like the one described in the scenario above have been commonplace throughout my twenty years of leading worship. Of the hundreds of meetings for which I have led worship, there have been perhaps only a few where everything went exactly right. The truth is that many worship leaders have told me that they have never had even *one* service where everything went just right (and I thought *my* case of perfectionism was severe!).

I once heard well-known speaker Gary Smalley make a fascinating statement that really struck me. He said, "The number one cause of stress is unfulfilled expectations." Unfulfilled expectations. Like when the backup singers go off-key or when the bass guitar is causing a buzz in the sound system. Our expectations are that everything will go perfectly. And when they don't, the obvious result is exactly what Smalley said: stress.

Let's be realistic. As long as we live in this world, as long as we deal with people, there will always be problems. There will always be mistakes. Not everything will go perfectly. The sooner we realize this, the sooner we will begin to overcome the perfectionism affliction.

I am not advocating that we stop doing our best. God is worthy of the very best we can give. However, "He knows how we are formed, He remembers that we are dust" (Psalm 103:14). God knows that we will make mistakes and that those around us will make mistakes. Fortunately, that's where His grace comes in. When the level of perfection that we expect doesn't happen, His grace is still sufficient.

Over the years I have been amazed at what God has done through services that were seemingly riddled with errors. When we did most things wrong, the Lord still, like the people said of Jesus in Mark 7:37, "has done all things well."

In spite of us, God is always faithful. Recognizing the fullness of His faithfulness and grace has helped me to start to live beyond the perfectionism syndrome. I still always endeavor to put forth the best possible effort, but the results are His responsibility. And if I am tempted to think that "everything went wrong," I simply trust His grace.

Karen Lafferty

Karen Lafferty is probably best known in the Christian world as the author of the Scripture chorus "Seek Ye First." This chorus has been key in opening doors to take her music around the world. Karen helped  *pioneer contemporary Christian music during the Jesus Movement in the 1970s as one of the first musicians with the California-based record company Maranatha! Music.*

As Karen's ministry led her outside of the U.S., she began to see the incredible potential of using contemporary Christian music to reach youth for Christ. In 1980 Karen founded Musicians For Missions International (MFMI) as part of Youth With A Mission (YWAM) in Amsterdam, Holland. The activities of MFMI have ranged from short-term mission trips to full-time staff "musicianaries" to a School of Music in Missions as part of YWAM's University of the Nations.

Karen returned to her U.S. home in 1996 and now directs MFMI from Santa Fe, New Mexico. Today, after nearly four decades in Christian music, Karen continues to have much vision to train and mobilize musicians, lead worship, minister through concerts, write and record songs, and encourage others to "seek first the kingdom of God."

SIMPLE PRAISE SIMPLY DRAWS PEOPLE TO JESUS

by Karen Lafferty

It was April 1979 when I found myself in Athens, Greece, with about two hundred other young people from fifteen different countries. Each of us had been part of a Youth With A Mission (YWAM) Discipleship Training School (DTS) somewhere in Europe. My DTS was in Holland. Just a few days earlier I had arrived in Athens after a five-day bus trip with the other DTS students for the outreach phase of our school.

Having already been in a full-time music ministry for eight years, I now felt the Lord was leading me to focus on using music in missions. During a three-month tour of Europe in 1978, I had seen firsthand that contemporary Christian music and worship were powerful tools to reach young people for Christ worldwide. It was amazing to me that even though I sang in English instead of their native European languages, the youth would sit through a two-hour concert and often respond to the gospel message at the end. I became convinced that the primary reason for their interest was that I was doing a musical "style" they enjoyed. In reality, though, our strongest link was our human need to know and worship our Creator. As I spoke about Christ through an interpreter and presented my songs, the Holy Spirit would speak to the hearts of the people. And now here I was in Athens, asking God to once again use me to reveal Him to the people, this time the Greek people.

The Lord had already used the "internationalness" of my DTS to teach me many new things about music ministry and worship. The Europeans had encouraged me to play my oboe with the worship team. I had played it only with orchestras. What a joy to learn how to make my oboe an extension of my heart in worship of the Lord. I was also learning how sounds that had been so foreign to me, like *Heer*, which means "Lord" in Dutch, were taking on a heart meaning to me as I worshiped with the Dutch Christians.

It seemed like a normal outreach day as we headed out en masse to support the performance of "Toymaker and Son," a colorful pantomime that portrays the gospel. However, we soon realized that God wanted to touch the people of Athens in a different way that day. The Athens police decided we could not perform "Toymaker and Son" on the Athens University steps, even though we had done it on several previous days. We were all very disappointed but asked God what we should do. This was the first time during the outreach that we decided we would split into smaller groups of about twenty and go to different parts of the city. I ended up with a group that simply stood in a quiet corner of a parking lot worshiping God in a very gentle manner. Even though our intention was simply to worship the Lord, not necessarily to draw a crowd, people began to come closer as they heard the songs of praise.

As the people gathered I thought of Jesus' heart when He saw the multitudes and felt compassion because they were distressed and downcast like sheep without a shepherd (Mark 6:34). We decided not to preach that day; rather we told people that we would continue to sing songs of worship because God said that He would inhabit the praises of His people (Psalm 22:3) and that in His presence is the fullness of joy (Psalm 16:11). We explained that God wanted them to experience His love and joy that day. I can't even recall how long we continued to worship, but I remember another verse coming alive to me—Psalm 40:3: "And He put a new song in my mouth, a song of praise to our God; many will *see* and fear, and will trust in the LORD."

As some of us continued to worship, our leader invited any who had felt the presence of the Lord there and who wanted to talk with one of us about Him to come forward. As many of them began to come forward to talk and pray with us, I once again saw how people long to be in God's presence. Worship can draw people into God's presence, even on the busy streets of a crowded city. It wasn't just the "style" of music that drew them but the Spirit that inhabited the music. We all witnessed firsthand how simple praise simply draws people to Jesus.

Charlie and Jill LeBlanc

Charlie and Jill LeBlanc have pursued the call of God on their lives to teach, encourage, and inspire by the Word of God through song. Traveling extensively, they have led congregations all over the world into God's presence through praise and worship.

Beginning their adventure into full-time ministry in 1980, the LeBlancs have fulfilled the spectrum of church staff positions, from worship leader to youth pastor to associate pastor. They have also led praise and worship for various ministries, including Joyce Meyer for seven years and Andrew Wommack from the mid-1980s to the present.

Charlie was the worship leader on two of Integrity's Hosanna! recordings, Lord of All *and* To Him Who Sits on the Throne. *Both Charlie and Jill were songwriters for and sang background vocals on several of Integrity's earlier recordings.*

One of Charlie and Jill's signature scriptures representing the heart of their ministry is Colossians 3:16: "Let the word of Christ dwell in you richly in all wisdom, teaching and admonishing one another in psalms and hymns and spiritual songs."

The LeBlancs live in St. Louis, Missouri, and are members of St. Louis Family Church.

THE HEART OF THE MATTER

by Charlie and Jill LeBlanc

Several years ago Jill and I were serving as worship leaders at a growing church in St. Louis, Missouri. During that time we experienced a great lesson in worship leading that has helped us to this day.

One afternoon the pastor came into my office to describe an exciting vision he had: to rent a large auditorium and combine both of our Sunday-morning services into one big, explosive gathering of all of the saints. We would call it "Super Sunday." As he continued to describe his ideas of bringing in a special musical guest, and possibly a drama presentation, I began to catch the vision. We continued to discuss all of the preparations that I would need to handle, including special songs to teach the band and worship singers and special practices for this great event. The work began with only one month lead time, so we worked very hard, planning and preparing continually.

Over the next few weeks the details were coming together in extraordinary ways. The entire worship team was excited about the special service, and my wife, Jill, and I were preparing our hearts for a really special time in leading God's people in worship.

The great day arrived after weeks of intense rehearsing. The band, singers, and sound crew all arrived at the auditorium very early for final sound checks. We all were excited and ready to go!

As was our custom, we met backstage for prayer and worship together about a half hour before the service started. I was a little nervous, since I had not seen the pastor yet. He normally would be there early with us, giving his last-minute suggestions and encouragement to the group, and then would join us in prayer. Nevertheless, we entered into a time of prayer and heartfelt praise together as the clock ticked all the way down to starting time.

The noise in the auditorium and a sneak peek every now and then proved that the room was rapidly filling up with not only our congregation from both Sunday services but also their friends and relatives. The place was jam-packed! Just as we said our "Amen," I saw the pastor walk in. Little did I know at the time that he had spent half the night in the hospital emergency room with a serious problem.

When the pastor and I finally connected that morning, he shared about the excitement in his heart regarding the service and asked if everything was ready. "Everything's great!" I responded. He asked if Jill and I were ready to lead the people in praise and worship. I assured him that we were as prepared as we could be. (Are any of us ever *really*, totally ready to lead in worship of the almighty Creator?!) The pastor then informed me that he would simply open the service, greet the people, and turn it right over to us for leading the praise and worship.

As we all got into our places, with instruments and microphones in hand, our pastor approached the podium to open the service. There was an obvious excitement among the people. Upon the pastor's first greeting of "Isn't the Lord's presence wonderful in this place!" everyone present erupted in praise and applause for the King of kings and Lord of lords. The faith and expectancy in the room was almost tangible! Sensing that the people were definitely ready to worship, our pastor responded by opening up with a song that he couldn't contain any longer: "Then sings my soul, my Savior God to Thee, how great Thou art, how great Thou art!" The congregation joined in with glorious worship from their hearts. It was so intense that it seemed as though even the angels had joined in with us!

When the chorus ended, another enormous eruption of praise broke out. Jill and I stood just behind the pastor and off to the side, microphones in hand, raring to go like a couple of racehorses. All of the wonderful new songs and the great band licks we had practiced were being rehearsed in my head as I waited for our pastor to signal us to come and take over. As the presence of the Lord powerfully filled the room, our pastor spontaneously took off into "We bring the sacrifice of praise . . . ," with the band running to catch up. Before I knew it, everyone in the place seemed to be worshiping—everyone except me. With a half-cocked smile on my face, I began to realize that something wasn't right on the inside of me. All these weeks of preparing to lead worship on this special morning were all of a sudden amounting to nothing. I knew that my heart was wrong, and in the midst of this celebration, the Lord and I had a little conversation.

"Lord, I know my heart is wrong. I need Your help."

"Charlie, why did you come here this morning?"

"To lead Your people into worship, and to worship You myself, Lord."

"Well, are the people worshiping?"

"Yes, Lord, but—"

He stopped me and said, "Then the mission is accomplished. Now, you just get your heart right and begin to worship Me."

This was a very difficult lesson to learn. You see, it really doesn't matter who is leading the worship. What matters is that we all worship Him!

After that experience a new level of freedom came into my life, a new joy to serve and help people come into God's presence, no matter what the situation might be. If I can help in any way, whether it be preparing the worship team, playing an instrument, singing background vocals, or leading the worship, it makes no difference, as long as the mission is being accomplished and God's people worship Him in spirit and truth (John 4:24).

Perhaps we should all make a new commitment to humble ourselves and submit to one another, preferring one another and serving each other, to see God's praises fill the earth.

Don McMinn

Don McMinn, PhD, serves on the staff of The Center for Marriage and Family Intimacy and is director of The Worship Connection. He is the

author of Entering His Presence, Strategic Living, The Practice of Praise, A Heart Aflame, *and* Spiritual Strongholds.

Don has also served as worship leader at several churches in Texas and Oklahoma. Most recently he was worship leader at the 12,000-member First Baptist Church in Del City, Oklahoma.

He received his undergraduate degree from the University of Texas at Austin and his doctorate from North Texas State University. He has a particular burden to teach principles of intimacy as they relate to our relationship with God and meaningful others.

Don and his wife, Mary, have two daughters and live in the Dallas/Fort Worth area.

CHILDLIKE HALLELUJAHS

by Don McMinn

~❧ **M**y assignment: teach a third-grade Sunday-school class for one week.

The topic: praise.

I love to teach, so that part of the assignment was inviting. I've been a student of worship for twenty years, so I love to teach on the topic of praise. But third graders?

When the third-grade Sunday-school teacher asked me to teach her class about praise, I couldn't say no. After all, I had written three books on the subject and was the worship leader of our church. But I was intimidated by the challenge of having to communicate to a group of eight-year-olds. Even after thinking about it all week long, I still had no idea of how to communicate the wonders of praise and worship to fidgety children.

I was hoping that the promise of Matthew 10:19 would apply to this situation: "Do not worry about what to say or how to say it. At that time you will be given what to say." And it did.

As I was walking up the stairs to the classroom, the Lord reminded me that the night before, the L.A. Lakers and the Boston Celtics had played game seven of the NBA Finals. It was one of those classic, down-to-the-buzzer games. In the final few seconds, Boston scored the winning basket. The game was being played in the Gardens, so you can imagine the crowd's reaction during those last few moments. In the first few minutes of postgame coverage, the television commentators didn't even bother talking. The cameras scanned the audience first, then the players, and then the audience again. The activity inside the stadium said it all: Boston had won, and those who savored the victory were celebrating.

The Hebrew word *halal* (transliterated, we get the word *hallelujah*) means "a spontaneous, unsolicited reaction to a joyful situation." When the psalmist says "Hallelujah!" he's not expressing a quiet, sober emotion. It's more similar to the emotions one would feel at the end of a championship basketball game when one's team has just won in the final seconds.

So here's what I did when I stood in front of twenty-five third graders to teach them about praise. After seating them on the floor, I asked how many of them had seen the championship game the night before. For the sake of those who hadn't, I retold, in great detail, the events of the last five minutes and, in particular, what went on after the game was over. After explaining the meaning of *halal,* I simply drew a correlation between the feelings of joy and celebration expressed by the fans of the Boston Celtics and the joy and celebration that should erupt from our hearts whenever we think of the wonderful victory that Christ has won.

I spent a few minutes reminding the children of how awesome, wonderful, and good God is. I also reminded them of how evil, devious, and hateful Satan is. Then I took them to the cross, where the battle of the ages occurred. God's best, His Son, pitted against the infamous hosts of hell. I told them about the greatest tactical wartime strategy of all time. I described how Satan, in attempting to kill the Savior, was nothing more than a pawn manipulated by the sovereign hand of God to secure the victory of His Son. The victory was so complete that "Having disarmed the powers and authorities, he made a public spectacle of them, triumphing over them by the cross" (Colossians 2:15).

One thing I love about children is their lack of restraint, their total absence of inhibition in expressing emotion. Perhaps that's why Jesus taught us to be childlike in our faith—not childish but childlike. Having set up the correlation between the celebration at a basketball game and the aura that a good praise service should have, I simply told the children that I was going to give a countdown from twenty to one, just like the fans do at the end of a basketball game. I told them that when I got to one, I wanted them to jump up and celebrate Jesus—because He had won the ultimate contest of the ages.

When the count was over, the children erupted into wonderful, joyful, spontaneous, and celebrative praise. They yelled, clapped, jumped up and down, and hugged each other. It was a sight to behold. God inhabited the praises of those children, and those few moments became for me an unforgettable experience.

Yes, a lesson on praise was taught that day, and I was one of the students.

Praise is simply acknowledging, honoring, and celebrating the person and work of Christ. In colloquial terms, praise is just bragging on Jesus.

My prayer is that God will grant me a boldness to unashamedly declare His great worth, both in the "sanctuary" and as a lifestyle. I pray for a childlikeness in my worship—that I'll be so caught up in the wonder of His majesty and grace that I won't worry about what others around me are or are not doing or what they're thinking about me as I express my love to God.

God, give us hearts to worship You in a great, childlike way.

Sally Morgenthaler

Sally Morgenthaler is recognized as an innovator in Christian practices worldwide. Since 1992 she has been pioneering new worship forms characterized by both cultural relevance and worship faithfulness. Her  *prophetic role among church leaders and local congregations continues to increase in denominational scope and impact as her work now broadens into the arena of new forms of leadership and the untapped potential of women.*

Known best for her book Worship Evangelism *(Zondervan, 1998), Sally became a trusted interpreter of postmodern culture and a guide to the crucial shifts the North American church must make if it is to become a transforming presence within pre-Christian communities. She has contributed to eight books. Her latest collaborative effort was* Exploring the Worship Spectrum: Six Views *(Zondervan, 2004), in which her chapter has been hailed as a "road map" to emerging worship.*

Sally has taught both graduate and undergraduate courses at many schools, including Yale University, Asbury Seminary, Denver Seminary, Fuller Theological Seminary, and Gordon Conwell Seminary. She has been a featured guest on radio stations around the country and a featured speaker at a wide variety of worship conferences. She also writes the worship and culture column for Leonard Sweet's PreachingPlus (www.preachingplus.com).

Founder of Sacramentis.com, Sally is an accomplished photographer, with published work with Hallmark and BeautyWay cards. Her children, Peder and Anna Claire, live close by in her home state of Colorado.

GOD CALLING. FOR HEAVEN'S SAKE, ANSWER THE PHONE.

by Sally Morgenthaler

As an almost three-year-old, I was absolutely mesmerized with the aging upright that dominated our family dining room. The old clunker was way past its prime, with dents in its dents and chips in its ivories the size of lima beans. Yet it was the most fascinating object in my world, a colossal magnet for my miniature hands. I fingered the keys each time I passed. Considering that the piano was situated between the kitchen and the rest of the house, I carried out this mischievous ritual umpteen times a day!

Sometimes I'd actually stop long enough to play in a more orchestrated fashion. One fall day my mother was washing the breakfast dishes when she heard me climb onto the narrow bench and plop myself into concert position. From the first smash of the keys, she knew this performance was going to be different. Every motion, every connection, was absolutely intense. Staccato blows landed one right after the other, first in the low register, then extending to the uppermost keys and down again. Again and again. My mother, wise woman that she was, figured out at least two things as I punished that poor keyboard: I'd probably had too much brown sugar on my oatmeal, but more important, I was inhabiting quite another place than the family dining room!

All of a sudden the fury stopped. My dimpled little legs dropped to the floor and bolted for the kitchen. Tugging on my mother's apron, I exclaimed, "Mommy! Mommy! Guess what?"

"What?" she asked, anticipating some new flight of child-ish fancy, totally unrelated to the fiery keyboard drama I'd cut short in mid-combustion.

What I said she could never have predicted.

"Mommy," I exclaimed, breathless, "God's going to take all the bad people off the earth."

"He is?"

"Yep. They've been really awful and don't love Him. But you know what?"

"No, what?"

"God's going to make a new place for everybody who loves Him, and they're going to go there. So it's going to be all right, isn't it?"

"Why, yes, sweetheart, it sure is."

And off I went, racing back to the piano to begin Act Two. No thunder and lightning this time. No earthquakes. Just caressing, flutelike sounds, probably a musical melange of every lullaby and every peaceful image contained in my almost three-year-old brain.

Decades later my mother still tells this story. She tells it the same way every time. It stands complete, one cosmic moment crystallized and suspended in her memory. Until a few years ago I disregarded her tale as pure fiction, a quaint piece of maternal nostalgia. Even if it were true, what was the point? Such a tiny, whimsical slice of my childhood couldn't possibly have any bearing on my life. Not surprisingly, I balked at wor-ship ministry years later, unwilling to accept what my mother had known all along: God had chosen me to do something for His kingdom that involved both music and the Word. This was something quite beyond my experience or human capacity to accomplish. The struggle was on.

Perhaps you can relate to this struggle. Maybe you've cov-ered your eyes from time to time so that you won't see the hand of God upon you. Maybe you've stopped up your ears so you can't hear God's clarion call on your life. Perhaps you were once commissioned as a worship leader. You became the "keeper of worship," and you officially accepted a sacred charge. Inside, however, you were a bit unsure. Now doubts are your daily bread. The thrill of beginning is gone. It's just Sunday to Sunday, program to program, and you're in a perpetual state of image tweaking lest anyone find out you don't know what in the world you're doing up there on that platform.

I guarantee, you're not alone. Many of us as worship leaders reject God's anointing. We feel so undeserving, so utterly inadequate to the task God has assigned to us. We act like Moses. We cry out to God, "I'm not the one You want. I'm not a leader. I'm only a musician, and a mediocre one at that. You made a mistake!"

Ah, but God doesn't make mistakes. What's more, God doesn't choose people according to *our* standards. We worship leaders would do well to memorize 1 Corinthians 1:26–29: "Think of what you were when you were called. Not many of you were wise by human standards; not many were influential; not many were of noble birth. But God chose the foolish things of the world to shame the wise; God chose the weak things of the world to shame the strong. He chose the lowly things of this world and the despised things—and the things that are not—to nullify the things that are, so that no one may boast before him."

Who of us can accomplish anything apart from God's hand? Without God's grace, without God's empowering, refining Spirit, who could stand? Who could even think of ushering people into the magnificent presence of the One who is, was, and is to come—the omnipotent, omniscient, holy God who created, redeemed, and now sustains the very essence of life? Is there anyone who, in and of himself or herself, is truly fit to wear the mantle of worship leader, to mentor and mold the worship life of an entire congregation? Of course not. Yet the news of the gospel is, God makes us sufficient. God does lavish, supernatural, beyond-imagining things through the unlikeliest of candidates—us.

Now when my mother tells the story of that September day long ago, I listen. I marvel at how God speaks, even to almost three-year-olds. I remember my earliest lessons and my thrill at being asked to accompany the elementary school Christmas programs (yes, they actually had them, once upon a time!). I see myself as a twelve-year-old playing for nursing home sing-alongs and county-fair fashion shows. I replay all those nervous teenage recitals, the contests won and lost. I see the rejection letter from the conservatory, ripped open and tossed on the floor. Then my mind drifts to an arm injury right before college and three years of remedial practice. I feel the sting of humiliation as if it were yesterday and see a defeated young woman, giving it all up, sealing her hope and her music books in a cardboard box. I hear the silence of the decade that followed. And I see that God was there, all the time. God still had a plan. I just needed to make myself available.

Twila Paris

Twila Paris comes from an amazing Christian heritage. Her great-grandparents were ministers of the gospel and moved across the Southern Plains in the early part of the twentieth century, setting up tent meetings and brush-arbor churches. Her grandparents were also pastors who started churches where none existed. As one church was  *planted and brought to the place of relative independence, they moved on to another place to repeat the process of building the church. Twila's dad is an ordained minister and for much of his ministry has worked with Youth With A Mission, working with people who carry the gospel all over the world.*

Because Twila was brought up in a family employed in an itinerant ministry, she was a "team" member as far back as she can remember. Her team job was to sing. Twila was the oldest of four children, and she began to solo sing in the team ministry by the time she was three. She cut her first record, called Twila Paris, America's Little Sweetheart, *at eight.*

Twila's worship songs like "He Is Exalted," "We Bow Down," and "Lamb of God" have had a major impact on churches worldwide.

EVERY HEART THAT IS BREAKING

by Twila Paris

❧ **M**y husband, Jack, has a good friend from college who got married shortly after we did. They keep up with each other as friends by going to dinner together every once in a while.

One night Jack's friend called and asked Jack to go to lunch with him the next day. Jack thought he sounded down in his spirits but didn't press him about it on the phone, figuring that if there was something wrong he would hear of it the next day.

As it turned out, the news was not good. Before a year had gone by in the marriage, Jack's friend's bride had decided that she did not love him and had simply packed up and left him without notice or reason.

Being a newlywed myself, I was sickened by the tragic circumstances of Jack's friend. That night my sleep was restless and full of pain, so I got up, went alone into my music room, and, in the early hours of the morning, continued to think about the pain Jack's friend was going through.

As I sat there meditating on the man's pain, I began to see the heart of God as it was turned toward Jack's friend and all the hurting people of the world. I know that God is fully aware of all the suffering that people go through and that God can bring comfort and healing to their lives.

I began to think of different examples of hurting people, and the song "Every Heart That Is Breaking" came to me. For every line in that song I have a personal example: the mother and young boy who had recently lost a husband and father, the fallen teenager and her devastated father, the son dying with AIDS, the hungry child, and the refugee. For them the message is that God sees them, and knows them, and loves them.

Worship ministers to the hurting people of the world because God is present in worship to bring a healing touch into people's lives. A lot of people say, "Don't go to worship to get, go to worship to give." I think that is a half-truth.

We do go to worship to give glory and honor to God. But worship is a two-way action. God is there doing what God has done for us in Jesus Christ. Through the death and resurrection of Christ, God has conquered all the powers of evil and will ultimately bring healing to all the nations and all the world. Right now, in worship, God gives us a taste of His healing, a down payment on our eternal treasure.

I think the church needs to be more sensitive to the hurting persons of the local congregation. I think the church needs to provide space within its worship for healing. It could be in songs, prayers, preaching, or communion or in a special act of anointing for healing. However a local church chooses to reach out to hurting people, a move in that direction is imperative.

Adapted from Twila Paris and Robert E. Webber, *In This Sanctuary* (Nashville, Tenn.: Star Song, 1993). Used by permission.

Andy Park

Andy Park was born and raised in the San Fernando Valley, a suburban area of Los Angeles. At seventeen, Andy came to a deeper relationship with Jesus Christ. Upon entering UCLA, he became involved in Bible studies and fellowship groups.

At the Vineyard Christian Fellowship in Reseda, California, Andy began his involvement in worship leading and songwriting. Andy  wrote and performed a variety of styles of contemporary Christian music. Through the early 1980s his focus began to shift more to writing worship songs. He moved to Langley, British Columbia, and joined the Langley Vineyard church plant, where he was on staff for four years as an assistant pastor.

In the 1980s Andy led worship for John Wimber conferences domestically and internationally and first recorded with Vineyard Music Group. He has since led worship on several Touching the Father's Heart series recordings, recorded an acoustic worship album, and has contributed to several of the Winds of Worship albums. Andy's songs include "The River Is Here" and "Spirit of the Sovereign Lord."

Andy and his wife, Linda, are the parents of six beautiful children: Zachary, David, Michael, Jessica, Benjamin, and Isaac.

FULFILL YOUR CALLING, NOT SOMEONE ELSE'S

by Andy Park

In my early twenties I served as an intern pastor in two different churches where the pastors were very gifted. Both pastors were skilled teachers and had the ability to draw large numbers of people through their teaching and charismatic personalities. At that point in my life I wasn't sure what I was supposed to do with my life. I thought maybe I was headed for full-time ministry, but when I compared myself with these gifted leaders, I couldn't see how I would make the grade in the ministry. I definitely was uncertain about how the particular mix of spiritual gifts God had given me would enable me to excel in pastoral work.

In those years I led small groups, taught Bible studies, counseled younger Christians, and led worship. I did reasonably well in these areas of ministry, but I wasn't setting the world on fire as an evangelist or drawing great numbers to the groups that I led. My greatest strength was always in the musical area, and I had lesser gifts in the other areas. I wanted to be faithful to use my gifts to their fullest potential to serve God, but I just didn't see how I could possibly fit into a church staff position. I also wondered whether my quiet personality would be a liability in my becoming a successful pastor.

In the midst of this time of struggling and soul searching, I was invited to join a church-planting team in Langley, British Columbia. My wife, Linda, and I had met Gary and Joy Best the previous summer on a ministry trip and had struck up a warm relationship with them. After checking out the area where Gary and Joy were planting the church and getting to know the leadership team, we decided it was the right thing to do.

In my staff position at Langley I majored in worship while working in various other areas of ministry. All of a sudden I found myself in an environment in which I thrived. I was encouraged to develop worship leaders for small groups and Sunday services. I enjoyed doing this. I met with some success, and I've been doing it ever since. I was amazed at the turn-around I had seen in my ministry in such a short period of time. Even though I wasn't a dynamic speaker with a magnetic personality, God was able to use me to impart the heart and skills required to be a worship leader.

This was the first of many experiences in which I've had to learn not to compare myself with other ministers. I was measuring my worth and calling as a minister against the gifts and callings that God had given to others. I began to see that all I had to do was minister in the gifts and strength He had given me. Take it from the apostle Peter: "Each one should use whatever gift he has received to serve others, faithfully administering God's grace in its various forms. If anyone speaks, he should do it as one speaking the very words of God. If anyone serves, he should do it with the strength God provides, so that in all things God may be praised through Jesus Christ. To him be the glory and the power for ever and ever. Amen" (1 Peter 4:10–11).

This scripture contains essential lessons for the worship leader. First, we all have different gifts. Although we can sharpen the tools God gives us, we can't determine what those tools are. Our tendency is to see a greatly gifted person and ask, "Why couldn't I have been given that ability?" Over and over again I marvel at the sovereignty of God—the way He calls and endows each person uniquely. Many times I've had to repent from jealousy of another's gift or position and realize that God is the boss. "There are different kinds of gifts, but the same Spirit. There are different kinds of service, but the same Lord. There are different kinds of working, but the same God works them in all men" (1 Corinthians 12:4–6). *He* is the only source of our gifts. If we forget that every good gift comes from God, we are liable to stand in awe of the gifted leaders around us instead of giving glory to God.

In this world where success is defined by climbing the ladder so that you can have great power and influence, we must reeducate ourselves according to God's values. According to Peter's exhortation, if we are faithful to give away whatever God has given us, we have found success. Success equals obedience. All I have to do is minister in the strength God provides for me, not the strength He gives to another. When we arrive in heaven and see Jesus, He won't ask us, "How many people did you minister to for Me?" He'll ask, "Were you faithful to use all the talents I gave you for My kingdom?"

My problem of comparing myself to others didn't stop with round one. As I was exposed to more worship leaders, I saw people with great expertise, either vocal or instrumental ability or skill in songwriting. In the midst of this I had a hard time not being envious of the things they could do. Confessing my weakness to God and others, I gradually learned to rejoice in the success of others and thank God for raising up other gifted people. God began to plant in me a generous, unselfish heart so that I could be genuinely happy when others around me were reaching new heights in worship leading. I don't think there was any magical moment in this process. It was simply a matter of being relentless to gain the heart of God and turn away from my self-centeredness.

It all comes into clear perspective when we "use whatever [gifts we have] to serve others, faithfully administering God's grace in its various forms" (1 Peter 4:10). I like to think of it as being a mail carrier. I pick up the packages at the post office and simply deliver them to the people. I can be careful in how I deliver the packages, but I can't really determine what's inside of them. I'm simply giving away whatever I get from God. He determines the size and contents of the gift.

Howard Rachinski

Howard Rachinski is President and CEO of Christian Copyright Licensing International (CCLI) and founder of the Church Copyright License, which helps churches comply with the copyright law. CCLI is currently  serving approximately 170,000 churches in Australia, Canada, New Zealand, the United Kingdom, the United States, South Africa, Europe, and Asia.

Howard has experience as a songwriter, arranger, record producer, and music sales manager and is recognized as an experienced seminar leader and contributing editor in music copyright law issues. His experience also extends to the local-church arena, where he was an associate pastor for seven years and a music minister for five years in one of the nation's largest churches, where he directed an eighty-voice choir and a thirty-piece orchestra.

Howard is recognized as an enthusiastic conference speaker, specializing in the areas of praise and worship, music culture, music ministry, and worship leading. Howard and his wife, Donna, live with their three children in Portland, Oregon.

A SMILE IN MY EYES
by Howard Rachinski

~ My nineteen-year-old daughter is currently experiencing that "struck by the lightning of love" syndrome that hits all of us sooner or later. She met her boyfriend during her first year of Bible college, and as is the case with an out-of-town college boyfriend, we get to see him in our house quite regularly for "feedings and washings."

It was during one of these visitations that I was able to observe a special phenomenon with my daughter. We were all in the family room, some reading books, others playing Battleship, and I was watching Ron Kenoly's video *God Is Able*.

"Isn't that something?" I said to my daughter, fully expecting her to be caught up in the same spirit as I. She did not respond. "Dyane," I called out to her. No response. "Dyane," I repeated a little louder. Still no response. "Dyane!" I yelled. Although she was no more than eight feet from me, she still did not hear me. Her boyfriend, hearing my repeated outbursts, softly spoke to her, "Dyane, your dad's calling you." She looked at me glazedly and said, "Yes, Dad?"

I had just observed two things. First, the only voice my daughter could hear was her boyfriend's. Second, she had a smile in her eyes. I then realized that as a worship leader, I had just finished observing worship and had received two very important insights.

When I lead worship, whose voice am I listening to? Have I made sure that my ear has been tuned to the One I love so that when He speaks I can respond? Have I heard His voice? Do I know what He has said His heart is for that specific time of worship? It is easy to try to lead worship the way others would tell you to, trying to adjust to comments of "too long," "too short," "too fast," "too slow," "too loud," "too soft." In the midst of the complexities of worship leading, I am reminded to stay in the simplicity of worship. When I am in His presence, His is the only voice I hear. Therefore, before I lead others in worship, I must be sure that I have first of all spent time in His presence.

Finally, what is in my eyes when I lead worship? Again, it is easy to get caught up in all the technical and professional aspects of worship leading. The design of our sanctuary makes it as difficult to lead worship as it is to fly a Boeing 747, and sometimes it is easy to feel like ranting and raving as a ringmaster at a circus. Manuals have been written about the importance and necessities of "emoting" when leading worship. Emotion without existence is a facade. Existence without emotion is death. If I am to praise Him who is the help (and health) of my countenance, then my countenance should be displaying the joy of being in His presence. When I think about the Lord, when I look upon His beauty, do my eyes light up? When I lead worship, do I have a smile in my eyes?

Bill Rayborn

William (Bill) H. Rayborn is president of TCMR Communications, Inc., and is editor and publisher of The Church Music Report, a newsletter for church musicians.

Bill is a native of Tulsa, Oklahoma, and a graduate of Oklahoma Baptist University, with a bachelor's degree in music education. He has served as minister of music at churches in Oklahoma, Missouri, South Carolina, Texas, and California. He was director of record promotion for Word, Inc., executive director of Andraé Crouch and the Disciples, vice president of Christian Artists Corporation, director of music publications for Tempo Music, and general manager of MSI Press.

Bill's hobbies include photography, computers, and music. He is married to the former Lynann Kurr, has four daughters, and resides in Grapevine, Texas, a suburb of Dallas/Fort Worth.

BE CAREFUL HOW YOU BUTTON YOUR COAT

by Bill Rayborn

While serving as minister of music at a church in South Carolina, I came to realize that as church music and worship leaders, we are being watched and people are following our example, no matter where we are.

It was a Sunday morning when one of our children's choirs was scheduled to sing. The mother of an eight-year-old choir member came to me before the service with a strange comment: "Mr. Rayborn, I hope you never do anything wrong."

I told her how much I shared her wish but asked why she would make such a statement. She then related this story:

It seems that they wanted their son to look his best for the choir program and had purchased a new suit for him to wear for the performance. As they got out of the car that morning, the mother asked the boy to button his coat. "Not right now, Mom," he replied. "I want to wait and see how Mr. Rayborn has his coat buttoned."

The Bible admonishes us to be an example for the believers. Those of us in leadership positions in the church need to understand we are being watched at all times. We need to be careful how we button our coats.

BEULAH LAND

by Bill Rayborn

One of my most favorite stories was told by Dr. Travis Shelton, professor at Southern Methodist University. Dr. Shelton tells how, while directing the music at his church, he frequently had a request service as part of their congregational singing. One woman in his congregation was always first with a request—and it was always the same request: "Beulah Land" (actually "Dwelling in Beulah Land").

Dr. Shelton says that one Sunday evening his choir was sitting at the front of the sanctuary when the woman made her regular request. He saw this as his chance to "teach her a lesson." In his very best dance-band style, he raced through the gospel song. The choir swayed from side to side, even raising their hands in mock Pentecostal fashion during the little afterbeat section of "Praise God." When the song was over, the choir laughed. Dr. Shelton was sure he had taught the woman a lesson and that "Beulah Land" would be a problem no more.

Two days later Dr. Shelton received two unsigned postcards, one of which he said "hangs over my desk to this day." The card said plainly: "Dear Dr. Shelton, 'Beulah Land' is here to stay. You ain't necessarily!"

There is a lesson to be learned here that goes far beyond "Dwelling in Beulah Land." We need to remember that we are servants of our congregations. While it could be argued that we should seek to expand the musical tastes (both up and down) of our people, we must never feel that it is our place to raise the musical level of our congregation. We need to meet our people's needs where they are!

This is probably one of the best arguments for the so-called blended service or blended worship. We need to give our people variety so that we can reach all of the people some of the time, not some of the people all of the time. Now, if you agree with this, let me add a word of caution. I've seen many allow the pendulum to swing too far one way. Just because praise and worship choruses appeal to many is no reason for a steady diet, thus neglecting some of the rich hymns, gospel songs, and anthems of the past.

So this is a plea for you to get to know your people and their needs—to do music that speaks to your people, not just to you. Don't allow your personal preferences to dictate your total direction. Otherwise you may find someone saying that their favorite songs are here to stay . . . and you ain't necessarily!

A TALE OF TWO CHURCHES
by Bill Rayborn

I recently received two church newsletters. Both were about the same size and appearance. Church number one, a church of about two thousand members in North Texas, carried a pastor's column in which, at the end of a lengthy epistle, the pastor, in just two sentences, offered congratulations to a pastoral staff member (not the minister of music) on his anniversary with the church.

Church number two, a church just slightly larger in Southern Florida, also carried a lengthy pastor's column, which took over two-thirds of an 8-1/2 x 11 page. Here the pastor raved about his minister of music in the entire column, titled "Not Duration, But Donation." He said, "Doing time is one thing, but it's the contribution of your life . . . ."

The minister of music at church number two had just celebrated his twentieth anniversary. The pastor wished him the best for their future years together. The minister of music at church number one was fired soon after—the fourth such firing of a pastoral member at that church in the past few years.

The moral I would suggest is that when you are in the process of choosing a position, you carefully consider not only the church, not only the salary, but also the history of the church and history of the senior pastor. Talk with former staff members both of the church and of the pastor's former churches *before* you accept the position.

While we need to be sensitive to God's calling from one church to another, He has given us intelligence to be able to learn from the past. It's been said that those who refuse to learn from history are destined to repeat its errors. This lesson can easily be applied to the church worship leader. After all, your future ministry and the future happiness of your family are at stake.

Robb Redman

Dr. Robb Redman is an author, teacher, and speaker. An ordained pastor in the Presbyterian Church (USA), Robb has a bachelor's degree from New College, University of Edinburgh, Scotland, and a doctorate 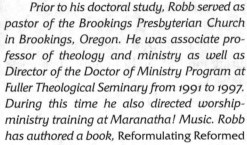 in theology from the University of Erlangen, Germany.

Prior to his doctoral study, Robb served as pastor of the Brookings Presbyterian Church in Brookings, Oregon. He was associate professor of theology and ministry as well as Director of the Doctor of Ministry Program at Fuller Theological Seminary from 1991 to 1997. During this time he also directed worship-ministry training at Maranatha! Music. Robb has authored a book, Reformulating Reformed Theology (University Press of America, 1997), and several reviews and articles, and serves as an editorial consultant for Worship Leader magazine.

Robb lives in San Antonio, Texas, with his wife, Pam. They have a St. Bernard named Clara and enjoy cooking, movies, reading, and exploring the Texas hill country.

A Pastor's Part in Worship

by Robb Redman

❧ **A**s a rookie pastor I learned a lot of lessons on the job for which seminary could not have prepared me. That's not the fault of the seminary. After all, how could it account for everything churches can throw at a greenhorn?

I cut my teeth as a worship leader strumming my guitar for the InterVarsity group at my college. Those were powerful times of praise and community. I don't know why, but I think I expected my first church to be like that group. As a result, I learned the hard way what's most important about introducing contemporary worship music to a traditional church.

In 1985, after just about a year on the job, I spent my two-week study leave at Fuller Seminary in Pasadena. One Sunday evening I visited the Anaheim Vineyard with Professor Eddie Gibbs. The worship music of the Vineyard was entirely new to me and very liberating. I bought all their tapes and sheet music. For the next several weeks I listened to the tapes and practiced. After discussing it with the session (the governing board of elders in the Presbyterian Church) we agreed to replace the opening hymn with new songs.

We took a big risk. When the organist finished the prelude, I put my guitar on over my Presbyterian pastor's robes and stepped up to the microphone. I looked goofy, but I didn't care. I was so enthusiastic about these songs and the authenticity of worship they released in me. I described how I discovered them and my desire to lead the church in singing a new song to the

Lord. I taught the people by singing through the song once and then invited the congregation to join in. The response was positive. The 11:00 AM service went well too, though not quite as enthusiastically.

Afterward the elders encouraged me to keep the songs in the early service, which had a more informal atmosphere, but they thought the songs didn't belong in the later service. We were set. Long before people knew what to call it, we had a blended worship service. Soon a woman in the church began to sing and play guitar with me. We continued until I left the church to pursue doctoral studies at the end of 1986. People appreciated the fresh, personal approach of the music and the way the new songs counterbalanced the depth of classic Presbyterian psalms and hymns. My last service in that church was a Christmas service led by a full band.

What did I learn in the process? First, I learned the importance of my role in modeling worship for the congregation and giving people permission to worship. I didn't fully understand that back then. I believed in prayerful planning, but I generally thought of my role in the service as a preacher and liturgist. To me the choir and organist were the song leaders. I discovered that pastoral leadership can't be delegated. As goofy as I looked with my robes and guitar, it sent an unmistakable signal to the church: I was assuming responsibility for leading the praise of the people. There is no substitute for pastoral leadership in worship.

The other major lesson I learned is that the authenticity of worship did not depend on my performance. I was not a very good guitarist or singer, but the congregation, particularly at the early service, did not respond to my musicianship as much as they responded to my desire to worship God authentically. In other words, they wanted to go where I was going spiritually. Spiritual leadership is more important than musical leadership.

Randy Rothwell

Randy Rothwell is committed to a lifestyle of wholehearted worship and to helping others discover the same. Saved at the early age of four-  *teen, Randy soon discovered that his love for music could be used as a powerful tool through which God's great love and power would flow and draw others closer to Jesus.*

Randy was the guest worship leader on five Integrity Music worship albums and has produced several projects for the Wholehearted Worship label, including Wholehearted Hymns Volumes 1 & 2 *and the* Worship Digest Volumes 1 & 2.

He currently serves as the worship leader and Associate Director of Worship & Arts at Forest Hill Church in Charlotte, North Carolina.

Randy and his wife, Dana, have been in the music ministry for over 30 years and now make their home in the quaint little town of Waxhaw, North Carolina. Their latest project is a live worship record-ing entitled Forever Free, *which they produced with their home church worship team.*

Breaking the Sound Barrier

by Randy Rothwell

One of the major things that can affect the experience of corporate worship is the quality of sound. A full, rich and balanced mix can make a big difference. I personally love an excellent PA system, and nothing thrills me more than great sounding monitors. To hear my guitar sounding clean and crisp and to hear my voice sounding clear and strong helps me feel more confident and, quite frankly, more in control. However, more times than I can count, the Lord has used a sound system to help me understand that it is He who is in control of the worship, not I.

Often I find myself leading worship in various churches, conferences, and seminars where the sound system is much less than desirable. Perhaps even worse, the PA system may be excellent, but the person operating the sound system has no ear for music and has—to be kind—no earthly idea what he or she is doing. This can prove to be quite a distraction for me if I allow it to be.

Sometimes when I arrive at a church and assess the PA system, my heart sinks. I begin to think that the worship time is not going to be what it could be because of the sound quality. This has frequently caused me to have the attitude of not giving my best to the people in the meeting. It has taken me a long time to finally realize that what the people really desire is to experience the Lord's presence in a fresh and powerful way and to leave the gathering feeling that they have been unified and have drawn closer to God.

I recall a particular event that happened when I was a teenager and a brand-new Christian back in the early '70s. In my hometown of Paducah, Kentucky, the church that I attended was made up of mostly teenagers, like me, who were newly saved and excited about Jesus Christ.

One night when we came to church, the late Keith Green, a very popular Christian musician at the time, was there. Our pastor had heard that he was touring in the Southeast and had somehow persuaded him to make an appearance at our small gathering. You can imagine the excitement of having such a nationally known Christian artist come to our small town. Needless to say, this was not a normal performance stop for him. The crowd was much smaller. The building was smaller. I imagine the honorarium was much smaller. Of course, the sound system was much, much less than that to which he was accustomed. In fact, we had the old Shure Vocal Master column speakers, which I affectionately referred to as the Shure Vocal Smasher!

Keith came in and got the best sound he could out of the PA and then just went on. I was struck by his confidence, his complete abandonment to God, and his joy in the presence of the Lord. He didn't just sing and entertain; he really worshiped. I felt united with him and all my brothers and sisters as we worshiped the Lord together. It was a very special time.

How different that night would have been if Keith had allowed himself to be distracted and annoyed by the limitations of our sound system.

I think about this in relation to my own worship-leading experiences. After I have rehearsed and gotten the best sound check I possibly can, I simply need to go forward and stay focused on the Lord, no matter what the natural circumstances may be. I have learned that the majority of folks in the congregation are totally oblivious to most of the little things that I find distracting and annoying. I must stay focused and trust

God to minister to each heart. After all, He is God (duh!). We need to give up our right to be in control and allow the grace and power of God to take over.

Gary Sadler

Gary Sadler is a songwriter and musician called to encourage authentic, wholehearted worship in the body of Christ. A prolific writer, he has penned many well-known worship songs (over ninety recorded on Integrity Music projects alone), and he continues his quest for fresh,

passionate expressions of praise to God. Some of his songs include "Ancient of Days," "I Rejoice in Your Love," "He Will Come and Save You," and "Wind of God." He was the worship leader on the Hosanna! Music recording King of the Ages. *Along with his writing, singing, and producing, Gary leads worship and teaches at various worship conferences and seminars.*

Gary enjoys all kinds of outdoor activities, including mountain climbing, rappelling, hiking, mountain biking, cross-country skiing, and fly fishing. He lives in Franklin, Tennessee, with his wife, Debra, and their two teenage daughters, Leah and Sarah, and their Wyoming cow dog, Sam.

Worship in the Hard Places
by Gary Sadler

So there I was. Banished from paradise (Jackson, Wyoming) and living in an area I had referenced on numerous occasions to be the one place I would never live. And it pressed in on me like heavy-duty pliers. The pace of a very driven city (you can see it in their eyes on the highway). The death of my parents. A threatening lawsuit. Confusing crossroads. Sickness. Intricate complications that Agatha Christie couldn't have thought up. And worse, far worse: we drove up and there was a big "No Peace" sign out front. We saw it everywhere we went, throughout the entire city, in every store, in every restaurant, church, and home, worn like a sticker on a hat by every person we met: "No Peace, not here, not for you." You might be asking right now, "What does this have to do with relating a significant, insightful event in a worship setting?" Everything!

It's just that I knew so much. I knew that worship had actually very little to do with music, that our true worship was a life simply given to God, lived out for His glory and purposes. I knew how to write worship songs. I knew His favor, and I knew His peace. I had even developed a well-received teaching called "Warfare from the Place of Peace." Peace was within me, running through the deepest parts of me, and I and my family danced within its walls of protection for years. Peace was what I was all about. Nothing was going to take my peace away.

But where was my peace now? How had it been stripped from me so quickly and so thoroughly, without warning? A Pearl Harbor of the soul! I went to bed every night with butterflies in my stomach, only to awaken in the morning with them still flying around down there. Zeros. Still bombing me senseless. My defenses were all down. I had been utterly defeated before I could even fire a shot. Peace sank to the bottom and settled in the mud. I remember realizing one day, "God has brought me to a hard place" (duh!). It was all around me, physically, spiritually, and circumstantially. Yeah, that's what was going on all right. I was Lot, being vexed in Sodom for a while. God would soon send a couple of angels to get us out of this mess. They'd see. A righteous man and his family in a proud, ambitious land. Bring down the fire! I called for the brimstone to make this town disappear from our memories. Wipe this mistake, this obvious error in sound judgment, from our slate and take us back to the wild, wide-open spaces. Rescue us from this hard place, O Lord! Take us back so we can worship You. That was the cry of my heart.

It was after about a year of this that the night sessions began. You know, those times when you're wakened out of a sound sleep to find the Spirit of God speaking to you. You are both glad about it and terrified at the same time. What He says goes straight into your being, without hindrance, without rational opposition. So as you lie there, God says, "Worship Me in this place." That same thing I had heard Him say twice in Jackson, Wyoming. It was so easy then out there. But this was now, and it was here, in Nashville, which I had come to view as a sort of purgatory, only worse.

God would speak, and I would remember: How I used to love to draw near to Him all by myself. How my heart would find the wind and the water and the wild, open places, the ranges in which I found room to run free. That place had always been in Him. The best thing in my life had been His presence, and it had been so long since I had gone there. I found myself reeling from the realization that the hard place wasn't in the terrible times or circumstances. The hard place wasn't in Nashville. The hard place was within me!

I know, I know, I still haven't said anything about a specific worship event. But I'm not finished. It has been about another year since all of this took place. My family and I still live in the Nashville area. We still have reservations about calling it home, because it still doesn't feel like home. Not yet. Life isn't perfect or even what it used to be. But God is here, and we worship Him in this place. He is doing new and wonderful things, breaking old boxes and starting fresh fires. In finding that truth, our perspectives have been altered.

I heard Rick Pitino, head coach of the Boston Celtics, say recently that he has two choices when he gets out of bed each day. He can be depressed and wonder why he was so crazy to have left such a cushy job at the University of Kentucky, with a winning basketball program, with all of its perks. Or he can be grateful for the opportunity to meet yet another challenge head-on, to restore the legendary Celtics program to championship form, and to see what happens. It is all perspective for him. His perception of what life holds for him makes the difference.

God has a vision for us—a picture of all we are to be in Him. He knows what it takes to break us, to mold us, to change us. I have begun to see the challenges as an extension of His mercy to me and my family—an opportunity to live on the edge and see what happens. Who wants to go to his or her grave bored to death, anyway? So we have chosen to have an adventure. We now see (along with many other worshipers here) that God wants to make a move in this town that will affect all the nations. He wants to influence the influencers. He wants to do such a new thing, kindle such a hot flame, that the little religious people within us all are annihilated, consumed by the revealed glory of a furiously zealous God. I love that God is doing the "things that we did not expect" (Isaiah 64:3). I love that He is blasting out of the theological cave we placed Him in.

So what does all this have to do with a worship event in my life? As I said before: everything. What He has done in my heart the past two years has affected everything in my life, including my expression of worship and the awareness of His presence and favor in those specific times. He reminds me that for any worship event to be real or significant, there must be something real and significant going on in the real world of our lives. He makes me recall that our songs merely reflect and express who He is and what He is doing and simply provide an environment in which He can do even more. In my worship times I am made very aware of how He has shown His loving kindness to me, and it humbles me. He has changed me. He is not finished, of course (I would hate to be left like this), but He has been pounding away day and night. There is a fire in me that until now had never burned. Not this fire. There is an eagerness to be changed and to believe that He *will* do the impossible in our land, in our day. He is getting us ready for His next, great move. New wine demands new wineskins.

I now know that He brought me to a hard place to show me the bitterness, the fear, the sin that was there, inside of me. He's doing a work He could never have done within the comfortable realm of paradise. He is sending the wind and the water to me. I run free in the wild, open places. I am living in the place of peace once again. That place is in Him.

Bob Sorge

Through the gleanings of his own personal crucible, Bob Sorge brings to the body of Christ a message of faith and hope that empowers believers to finish their race. Author of the widely acclaimed Exploring  Worship, *Bob has written numerous books that are largely the product of his own spiritual journey. Among his most noted works are* The Fire of Delayed Answers; Pain, Perplexity, and Promotion: A Prophetic Interpretation of the Book of Job; *and* Secrets of the Secret Place. *His most recent releases are* Following The River: A Vision for Corporate Worship *and* Unrelenting Prayer.

Bob served for thirteen years as senior pastor of Zion Fellowship in Canandaigua, New York. He now bases his writing and traveling ministry in Kansas City, Missouri, where he lives with his wife, Marci, three children, and two grandchildren.

Bob carries a passion for intimacy with Jesus that characterizes his life and message.

WORSHIP IS NO SWEAT

by Bob Sorge

It was over a decade ago that I attended my first worship conference. I still remember the sense of awe I felt as I experienced a form and depth of worship that was entirely new to me.

I came home from that conference with my eyes nearly popping out with vision for what God could do in and through the worship life of my home church.

My church knew immediately that I was different. There was a new passion, a new intensity—and also a form of expression that was new to our church. My zeal to see change was graciously tolerated for a year. Then came the confrontation.

The pastor called me into his office and told me that the elders had talked about my worship leading. They had all agreed that they didn't like the way things were going and that I needed to make some changes. I was young and inexperienced and deeply mortified at the chastisement.

I approached the elders on an individual basis. I asked what they perceived to be the problem and what I should do about it. Each one gave me a totally different answer! "Not enough hymns." "Too many fast songs." "We're in a rut." I came away with my head swimming and cried out, "Lord, what is going on here?"

Then the Lord helped me to see the common denominator in all the elders' responses as He spoke gently to my heart: "You're striving in the flesh." I realized that I had succumbed to using my natural strengths in trying to implement a godly vision. I was definitely being drawn forward by the Spirit, but in my zeal to see the people enter into the freshness of what God was doing, I had begun to push on the thing with my soul.

The Lord began to teach me how to release a worship service to Him and not get all uptight about whether it was meeting my expectations. To bring me to a place of balance, the Lord actually had to get me to the place where I didn't really care at all about how the worship service went—I just put my eyes on Jesus and enjoyed Him and left the worship service up to Him. I discovered that it worked. The people still worshiped, even when I took a less aggressive posture. Whereas I used to come away from leading a worship service with my shirt soaking, I learned during this time that "worship is no sweat."

I still have to release to the Lord every worship service I lead. How I long to see a dynamic release of praise and worship in the congregation. But I've learned to take my hands off the service and surrender to the genuine prompting of the Holy Spirit. I've continued to grow in this ever since that time about twelve years ago when my pastor took on the willingness to confront.

Tommy Walker

Tommy Walker is currently the worship leader at Christian Assembly Foursquare Church in Los Angeles, California. He has written such songs as "Mourning Into Dancing" from Ron Kenoly's Hosanna! Music

recording Lift Him Up *and "Lord, I Believe In You" from Crystal Lewis's latest release,* Gold.

Tommy has been the key worship leader for Promise Keepers stadium events, Greg Laurie Harvest Crusades, Luis Palau's El Paso, Texas, 1997 Crusade, and many others. Tommy has written songs for these crusades such as "No Greater Love," "These Things Are True of You," and the new chorus arrangement of the great hymn "A Mighty Fortress Is Our God," which was sung at Promise Keepers' Stand in the Gap in Washington, D.C. He recorded a live album for Maranatha! Music in 1994 and has written and sung many other songs for them as well.

Tommy is currently involved in taking worship evangelism to various parts of the world with the CA (Christian Assembly) Worship Band, leading people to Christ, giving to the poor, and training worship leaders throughout the world. He has also recorded four albums for his church's independent label, Get Down Records.

You Can Do It, Tommy

by Tommy Walker

∼≪ I'm the last of six kids in my family, all of whom were somewhat musical. I, though, pursued music with a passion my whole life. Because of this, I was given opportunities to lead worship in different youth groups at a very young age. However, I usually found I was extremely nervous—the kind of nervous that makes everyone else nervous and definitely can hinder worship.

Then one day as I was talking to my mom, she told me something I've never forgotten. She said, "Tommy, throughout my whole pregnancy with you, I prayed every day that God would give me a musician, someone who would give glory to God through music." I know it sounds simple, but what this said to me was that God created me for this. Before I was even born, He was knitting in me abilities to usher people into His presence.

I think a number-one enemy of worship leaders is a lack of confidence. This is certainly an issue I have had to deal with continually. The way I've begun to overcome this problem is by letting God tell me something I heard Him say after talking to my mom: "You can do this, Tommy. I created you for this."

One instance I'll never forget was in May of 1997. I was given the incredible and undeserved privilege of leading a stadium full of men at a Promise Keepers event. As I was walking onto the stage, I remember feeling terrified and thinking, *This is definitely over my head. How did I ever get myself into this?* I quickly recited one of my favorite verses, 1 Peter 2:9, and whispered it in first person to myself: "I'm a chosen person, in a royal priesthood, and part of a holy nation. I belong to God, that I might declare His praises."

After I prayed that, God whispered those words to me again: "You can do this, Tommy. I created you for this." After the first song was counted off and we got things rolling, a joy came over me that was so deep I could hardly breathe. I couldn't help but picture my mom sitting in a rocking chair praying for me as I was still in her womb.

Letting God remind me that He chose me and that He put these abilities in me has enabled me to do things far beyond what I could have ever dreamed, and in the process I've been able to give Him even more glory wherever He has taken me!

THE STOPPING QUESTION: WHAT IF I MUST?

by Tommy Walker

I was recently in the Philippines doing what we call a "Worship Evangelism Concert" and experienced something they never taught me in worship leader school. What do you do if the crowd won't let you end the song? This is a good problem to have.

At our gathering, the people were joyfully clapping along with the rhythm of the song. Every time I tried to end it, they wouldn't stop clapping. Basically what I learned that night was, if something is working and ministering, don't stop. We repeated the song in every way possible for about twenty minutes, taking instrumental solos, singing it a cappella, etc. It was an incredible time! If I had stopped the song when planned, the momentum we had gained through that experience would have been nowhere as great.

Many years ago I had a similar situation that went the other direction. I was leading worship at my church and started a song in much too high a key. The song had a big range, so everyone knew that when we got to the chorus it was going to be all over. You have to understand, this was a ballad in the midst of what was supposed to be a serious moment. Well, I in my lack of experience thought I should pretend everything was cool and just go for it. When the chorus came, my voice cracked, and I couldn't even come close to reaching the high notes, much less expect the congregation to hit those notes. Everyone finally just started laughing. Of course, I had my eyes closed, pretending there was no problem. When I opened them, I realized the people were basically laughing at me.

What I learned from this worship disaster was to loosen up a little bit and fix something early on, before it is too late. Since then I've made the same mistake but quickly changed the key before the chorus or just stopped the song altogether and simply told everyone what I was doing and started it up again. The moral to this story is that if something isn't working, don't keep going and make people suffer through it. It's much better to stop and begin again.

Kelly Willard

Kelly Willard started in music ministry at the tender age of thirteen. It was then that she regularly visited nursing homes and participated in Sunday and weekday services at her home church in Winter Haven, Florida. She also began writing songs at that time. In the years to follow

she found herself playing piano and singing in various gospel and contemporary Christian music groups, such as The Archers and Harlan Rogers & Friends.

It was not until she was twenty-two years old and had been married for four years that her first solo recording, titled Blame It on the One I Love, *was made and released by Maranatha! Music.*

Kelly has subsequently done several other solo projects. All along the way Kelly has enjoyed what she considers "giving my gifts freely back to the Lord by supporting my fellow Christian artists," as she has gladly participated when asked to sing duets or background vocals. In this capacity she has joined such artists as Twila Paris, Paul Overstreet, Ricky Skaggs, and Buddy Green. Additionally, she has sung on many Maranatha! Music Praise recordings and Integrity's Hosanna! Music Praise projects.

Kelly attends Belmont Church in Nashville, Tennessee, and frequently assists in worship leading there. Kelly and her husband, Dan, live in the Nashville area and have two children, Bryan and Haylie.

YOU CAN ONLY LEAD WHERE YOU ARE GOING

by Kelly Willard

In my early years of ministry I honestly did not realize that I led people into worshiping God. All I knew was that out of my own personal need and desperation, I sang my songs directly to the Lord. I never really knew the impact my singing had on people until I began to hear back from them (a few here and there) the stories of the effect my voice and songs were having on their relationships with God. That to me was a great blessing, but it also presented a great challenge for me from that time forth.

The challenge has been for me to be sure that I don't consciously try to "move" people by my singing, lest I enter into emotionally manipulating people, which I consider "spiritual witchcraft." I have discovered that my real role in leading people into the worship of God is to go there myself, just as I had always done before I became aware of the effect my personal worship had on others. To confirm this fact, I remember the Holy Spirit once speaking very specifically to my heart.

We were attending Newport-Mesa Christian Center in Costa Mesa, California, several years ago. One particular Sunday evening I was asked to sing. As I was trying to prepare my song list for that night, I distinctly sensed the Lord impressing an instruction upon my heart and mind. He said, "I want you to begin to sing more of the worship choruses that you love to sing so much anyway. You just focus on Me, love and worship

Me, and while you are singing, I will be doing things in people's hearts that you know not of. This is your part from now on."

This has been my constant endeavor ever since. I am convinced that you cannot take someone with you to a place that you are not going yourself. For me to be *leading* in worship, I must be worshiping the Lord myself.

I have also found that it is not our responsibility as worship leaders if someone does or does not choose to go with us into the Lord's presence. Our part is to go before the Lord in sincere love and adoration of Him. Those who witness that and want to come along will do so. (This revelation has relieved a major amount of stress from my worship leading!)

Worshiping God and leading His people into His presence is the greatest pleasure and privilege I know.

Darlene Zschech

Darlene Zschech has made music an integral part of her life since she was a child. From the age of ten she performed in a weekly children's  *television show, singing, dancing, and hosting segments. As a teenager Darlene continued in music, fronting various gospel bands in Brisbane, Australia.*

With considerable session experience, Darlene has worked on numerous commercials. Some of her most often played include commercials for McDonald's, Special K, KFC, and Diet Coke.

A prolific songwriter, Darlene wrote the well-known song "Shout to the Lord," which was nominated for song of the year for the 1998 Dove Awards. Her album by the same title was nominated for album of the year for the 1997 Dove Awards.

Darlene is lead vocalist, worship leader, and coproducer of Hillsong Music Australia's best-selling albums God Is in the House, All Things Are Possible, *and* Touching Heaven, Changing Earth.

For the past twelve years Darlene and her husband, Mark, have been a vital part of the leadership team at Hills Christian Life Centre in Sydney, Australia, where Darlene is the worship pastor and oversees the creative ministries department.

PRAISE THROUGH PAIN
by Darlene Zschech

Some time ago I was leading worship at a church in Texas. During the service my attention was drawn to a particular young couple who were visibly basking in the presence of God. Throughout the worship their faces were radiant. They seemed to be worshiping God with everything they had. I knew even then that I had to meet them. I was interested to know what caused such fervent worship of God.

When we did meet, I asked them about their love for God. I wanted them to share something of their testimony with me. As they began, they held hands and related how just six weeks earlier they had lost their five-week-old baby to crib death. That was certainly not what I was expecting to hear!

The couple were a living, breathing testimony of Exodus 15:2: "The LORD is my strength and my song." Their faith and worship were a declaration of God's power and lordship over their lives. Through their attitude of praise, God was able to minister to them and hold their lives together.

I will never forget this family. Their testimony and uncompromising faith in God has stirred and challenged the lives of many Christians. We are created to worship. However, it is not always easy when your world seems to be falling apart. When we start to sing and praise God, we are choosing to lay aside the problems of our lives. Instead, we lift our voices and our hearts to the One who ultimately holds our lives in His hands.

I clearly remember one morning just after my father passed away. I was hanging out the wash (some things in life just never change!), and my heart was breaking. My father was a wonderful man, and even though I knew he was now dancing with the angels, I missed him so much I found it hard to breathe. Because of this I started to sing, just quietly to myself, "To God be the glory . . ." (one of my father's favorite songs). I sensed the presence of God envelop me anew. There, while I was standing in my yard with my two-year-old running around by my feet, the Lord was touching my life. There was a wonderful healing in my heart that day.

Melodies and music have a dynamic ability to involve your soul, to connect with your heart, emotions, and mind. There is a power for life that is found only as we set our focus on the Lord and worship Him.

Adapted from Darlene Zschech, *Worship* (Hillsong Music, 1996). Used by permission.

Contributors

Leann Albrecht
www.leannalbrecht.com

Mark Altrogge
Lord of Life Church, Indiana, Pa.
www.forevergratefulmusic.com
www.sovereigngraceministries.org

Paul Baloche
www.leadworship.com

LaMar Boschman
www.worshipinstitute.com

Steve Bowersox
Bowersox Institute of Music, Jacksonville, Fla.

Scott Wesley Brown
www.scottwesleybrown.com

Geoff Bullock
www.geoffbullock.com

Terry Butler

David Butterbaugh

John Chevalier
Moriah Ministries (www.moriahministries.com)

John Chisum
Firm Foundation Worship Ministries
Worship4Life (www.worship4life.org)

Phil Christensen
www.thronetogether.com

Curt Coffield
www.helpingothersworship.com

Lindell Cooley
Music Missions International (www.mmi-inc.com)

Tommy Coomes

Shawn Craig
PCD Ministries (www.phillipscraiganddean.com)

Danny Daniels
www.danny-daniels.com

Kirk and Deby Dearman
Come to the Quiet Ministries (www.cometothequiet.com)

Lynn DeShazo
www.lynndeshazo.com

Brian Doerksen
www.briandoerksen.com

Eddie Espinosa

Darrell Evans
www.darrellevans.com

Bob Fitts
www.bobfitts.com

Rick Founds
www.rickfounds.com

Steve Fry
www.stevenfryministries.com
Messenger Fellowship (www.messengerfellowship.com)

Dan Gardner
Executive Pastor, Zion Christian Church, Troy, Mich.

David Garratt
Scripture in Song, New Zealand

Chuck Girard
www.chuck.org

Gerrit Gustafson
www.worshipschools.com

Dennis Jernigan
www.dennisjernigan.com

Bob Kauflin
www.worshipmatters.com

Monty Kelso
Southern California Worship Institute

Graham Kendrick
www.grahamkendrick.co.uk

CONTRIBUTORS

Bob Kilpatrick
www.bobkilpatrick.com

Tom Kraeuter
Training Resources, Inc. (www.training-resources.org)

Karen Lafferty
www.karenlafferty.com

Charlie and Jill LeBlanc
www.charlieandjill.com

Don McMinn

Sally Morgenthaler
www.trueconversations.com

Twila Paris
www.twilaparis.com

Andy Park
www.andypark.ca

Howard Rachinski
President and CEO, Christian Copyright Licensing International (CCLI)
(www.ccli.com)

Bill Rayborn
TCMR Communications, Inc. (www.tcmr.com)

Robb Redman

Randy Rothwell
Forest Hill Church, Charlotte, N.C. (www.foresthill.org)

Gary Sadler

Bob Sorge
Oasis House (www.oasishouse.net)

Tommy Walker
www.tommywalker.net

Kelly Willard
www.kellywillard.com

Darlene Zschech
www.darlenezschech.com

OTHER BOOKS BY TOM KRAEUTER

THE WORSHIP LEADER'S HANDBOOK
PRACTICAL ANSWERS TO TOUGH QUESTIONS
Tom Kraeuter, worship leader, worship seminar speaker, and author, tackles difficult issues involved in worship leading in an insightful, practical question-and-answer format. ISBN 1-883002-41-9

KEYS TO BECOMING AN EFFECTIVE WORSHIP LEADER
Practicing untried methods and ideas on a congregation or music team often proves discouraging—or even disastrous. This book offers practical, proven ideas gleaned from years of experience. ISBN 1-883002-06-0

GUIDING YOUR CHURCH THROUGH A WORSHIP TRANSITION
A PRACTICAL HANDBOOK FOR WORSHIP RENEWAL
Based on solid scriptural principles and the experiences of scores of churches, this practical resource equips congregations to negotiate change successfully. ISBN 1-932096-08-6

TIMES OF REFRESHING
A WORSHIP MINISTRY DEVOTIONAL
Seven of the most respected worship leaders today address topics close to the heart and essential to worship ministry. Written for individual or worship-team use. ISBN 1-883002-91-5

DEVELOPING AN EFFECTIVE WORSHIP MINISTRY
Practical, to-the-point teaching on developing a ministry of praise and worship within the local church. Kraeuter offers a solid foundation for churches pursuing contemporary worship. ISBN 1-883002-05-2

WORSHIP IS...WHAT?!
RETHINKING OUR IDEAS ABOUT WORSHIP
Worship practiced from a scriptural point of view affects the entire life of a believer as well as entire communities. Kraeuter invites his readers to enjoy the breadth and essence of biblical worship. ISBN 1-883002-38-9

ARE THERE TERRORISTS IN YOUR CHURCH?
The foremost attack on the body of Christ is coming from within. This power-packed book teaches how to identify "church terrorists" and how to stand against and diffuse the attacks. ISBN 1-932096-31-0

To purchase or for information, contact
Training Resources, Inc., 8929 Old LeMay Ferry Road, Hillsboro, MO 63050
636-789-4522 / www.training-resources.org

For more information about Emerald Books/YWAM Publishing, visit us online
at www.ywampublishing.com or call 1-800-922-2143.